Climate Crisis, Psychoanalysis, and Radical Ethics

Psychoanalysis engages with the difficult subjects in life, but it has been slow to address climate change. *Climate Crisis, Psychoanalysis, and Radical Ethics* draws on the latest scientific evidence to set out the likely effects of climate change on politics, economics, and society more generally, including impacts on psychoanalysts.

Despite a tendency to avoid the warnings, times of crisis summon clinicians to emerge from comfortable consulting rooms. Daily engaged with human suffering, they now face the inextricably bound together crises of global warming and massive social injustices. After considering historical and emotional causes of climate unconsciousness and of compulsive consumerism, this book argues that only a radical ethics of responsibility to be "my other's keeper" will truly wake us up to climate change and bring psychoanalysts to actively take on responsibilities, such as demanding change from governments, living more simply, flying less, and caring for the earth and its inhabitants everywhere.

Linking climate justice to radical ethics by way of psychoanalysis, Donna Orange explores many relevant aspects of psychoanalytic expertise, referring to work on trauma, mourning, and the transformation of trouble into purpose. Orange makes practical suggestions for action in the psychoanalytic and psychotherapeutic communities: reducing air travel, consolidating organizations and conferences, better use of Internet communication and education. This book includes both philosophical considerations of egoism (close to psychoanalytic narcissism) as problematic, together with work on shame and envy as motivating compulsive and conspicuous consumption.

The interweaving of climate emergency and massive social injustice presents psychoanalysts and organized psychoanalysis with a radical ethical demand and an extraordinary opportunity for leadership. *Climate Crisis, Psychoanalysis, and Radical Ethics* will provide accessible and thought-provoking reading for psychoanalysts and psychotherapists, as well as philosophers, environmental studies scholars, and students studying across these fields.

Donna M. Orange, PhD, PsyD, is a psychoanalyst and philosopher living in California. She teaches at the NYU Postdoctoral Program and the Institute for the Psychoanalytic Study of Subjectivity, New York. Her books include *Thinking for Clinicians* (2010), *The Suffering Stranger* (2011), and most recently, *Nourishing the Inner Life of Clinicians and Humanitarians* (2016).

Climate Crisis, Psychoanalysis, and Radical Ethics

Donna M. Orange

Routledge
Taylor & Francis Group

LONDON AND NEW YORK

First published 2017
by Routledge
2 Park Square, Milton Park, Abingdon, Oxon OX14 4RN

and by Routledge
711 Third Avenue, New York, NY 10017

Routledge is an imprint of the Taylor & Francis Group, an informa business

© 2017 Donna M. Orange

The right of Donna M. Orange to be identified as author of this
work has been asserted by her in accordance with sections 77
and 78 of the Copyright, Designs and Patents Act 1988.

British Library Cataloguing in Publication Data
A catalogue record for this book is available from the British Library

Library of Congress Cataloging-in-Publication Data
Names: Orange, Donna M., author.
Title: Climate crisis, psychoanalysis, and radical ethics /
    Donna M. Orange.
Description: Abingdon, Oxon ; New York, NY : Routledge, 2017. |
    Includes bibliographical references and index.
Identifiers: LCCN 2016009860 | ISBN 9781138124851
    (hardback : alk. paper) | ISBN 9781138124868 (pbk. : alk. paper) |
    ISBN 9781315647906 (e-book : alk. paper)
Subjects: LCSH: Environmental psychology. | Climatic changes—
    Psychological aspects. | Climatic changes—Social aspects.
Classification: LCC BF353 .O7185 2017 | DDC 155.9/15—dc23
LC record available at https://lccn.loc.gov/2016009860

ISBN: 978-1-138-12485-1 (hbk)
ISBN: 978-1-138-12486-8 (pbk)
ISBN: 978-1-315-64790-6 (ebk)

Typeset in Bembo
by Apex CoVantage, LLC

To my climate justice pilgrimage companions
at Pilgrim Place in Claremont, California,
in gratitude for your challenge and inspiration

Contents

Acknowledgments

Permission from Taylor and Francis LLC is gratefully acknowledged to reuse a few paragraphs from my *Nourishing the Inner Life of Clinicians and Humanitarians* (2016) in Chapters 1 and 4.

Permission from Taylor and Francis LLC is also gratefully acknowledged for reuse, with some changes, of material from D. Orange, "Whose Shame Is It Anyway?," *Contemporary Psychoanalysis*, 44 (2008): 83–100, reprinted by permission of the William Alanson White Institute of Psychiatry, Psychoanalysis and Psychology and the William Alanson White Psychoanalytic Society, www.wawhite.org.

Introduction

Psychotherapy, though more alert now to our responsibility to the world's most vulnerable people, more conscious of our solidarity with those who suffer, seems to be working largely in a bubble. Climate change has already, scientists tell us in the most urgent voices they can find, become an emergency, threatening to overwhelm all attempts to stem the primarily human-created disaster. Still we psychoanalysts work quietly and faithfully on, living as we always did, driving to work, flying to conferences, watering our lawns, eating and consuming mindlessly. Meanwhile, most political and financial leaders conspire to hide ominous truths, no longer simply inconvenient but dire, and we allow ourselves not to notice. Are we psychotherapists, even psychoanalysts who should perhaps do better, conspiring or colluding to sustain an environmental unconscious? Are we helping to silence the canary in the coal mine?

Though my recent work has extended itself beyond my professional homes in relational psychoanalysis—originally in psychoanalytic self psychology and intersubjective systems theory—(Orange, 1995) to address colleagues in all humanistic psychotherapies (Orange, 2010, 2011), and most lately (Orange, 2016), humanitarian workers more generally (nurses, teachers, aid workers, caregivers of all kinds), I return here to thinking with psychoanalysts and those influenced by psychoanalytic traditions and thinking. Having received extensive education and training, including mandatory personal analysis, to prepare us for our work, we have, I believe, also acquired responsibility to be leaders, moral if not scientific, in confronting the global crisis we are living. We possess the intellectual and communal resources to take on this responsibility. So far, however, we have been resoundingly silent.

Where are the psychoanalysts, we who, rightly or wrongly, consider ourselves intellectual leaders in psychotherapy and in understanding human motivation? Perhaps we have learned nothing from the example of Sigmund Freud, who, blinded by his passion for his work, his love for Enlightenment German culture, and his need to be as important as Copernicus and Darwin, could not see that he and his Jewish family, as well as psychoanalysis itself, faced mortal danger in Vienna in the late 1930s. He and his daughter Anna escaped to England (Young-Bruehl, 2008) at the last moment, but several members of his family perished in the massacre. In another strange example, a few years later in the London *Blitzkrieg*, during one of the British Psychoanalytic Society's furious disputes about the origins of hatred and aggression, Donald Winnicott noted their actual effects: "I should like to point out that there is an air raid going on" (Grosskurth, 1986, p. 321). At the next meeting the Society decided to establish procedures for continuing their arguments during bombing raids. Are we, too, so absorbed in our theories, and worse, in our theoretical and interdenominational disputes over who belongs and who does not, that we fail to notice that human-caused planetary warming threatens to destroy the world within which we practice our beloved profession? Have we learned nothing from the heedlessness of Freud and of the second generation of analysts? We say that all is grist for the psychoanalytic mill, but what if this crisis threatens the survival of the mill itself?

We psychoanalysts, together with our colleagues in other therapeutic areas, actually have a unique contribution to make in this crucial moment. We can help not only to refocus our own attention on the imminent threats to our own way of life, but to the world's most vulnerable people and to the earth which supports us all. In the best psychoanalytic tradition we can notice the forms of historical unconsciousness, the still-walking ghosts of the narrative unconscious (Freeman, 2012), keeping us insensitive to the suffering in which we are implicated and for which we are responsible. We can call out the more selfish of the defenses that keep us avoidant, and name the forms of traumatic shock that keep us too paralyzed to respond appropriately. We can help with the processes of mourning not only the remembered ways of life, but also the loss of many kinds of hope and certainty for the future. Learning from our colleagues in Christchurch, New Zealand, from Latin American climate justice leaders, from First Nations leaders in Canada and elsewhere, we can ask ourselves and each other—including our patients—what really matters in time of crisis, thus responding more creatively than our analytic forebears did. But we have no time to waste. In Bill McKibben's (2015, p. 41), words, "there no longer is any long haul."

This small book addresses not only my psychoanalytic colleagues, from whom I have learned almost everything I may be able to contribute here, but also all readers taking up the climate challenge with an ear for what a psychoanalytic sensibility may provide. Acknowledging that my points of view—admittedly held less lightly than I often elsewhere advocate—remain only the limited perspectives I have been able to cobble together from the place and time I write, admitting freely the severe limitations to my knowledge of science, engineering, sociology, and many disciplines relevant to my topic, hoping that my tone still invites others to think better than I have been able to do, I set out anyway, full of trepidation, hoping to find others for the journey. Together we may be able to find paths out of the magical thinking and evasions of our past and present, and into a shared future that will be simpler, humbler, more communal, more reverent toward our mother earth and toward each other.

The first chapter addresses the question of climate injustice, looking first at the crisis and at the scientific consensus, asking whether or not the "developed" nations of the world can actually make the changes needed radically enough and quickly enough to limit the damage and keep our planet livable. Next, we consider what basic attitudes, in Europe and North America, have brought us to this crisis, and have kept it hidden from us. Next, we ask how and why the questions of climate change and social justice are inextricably linked, and what solutions become necessary or ruled out due to this linkage. Climate justice theorists agree that we must adopt no solutions to our current emergency except those that improve the lot of the poorest and most vulnerable people. Keeping intact the way of life of those already living luxuriously cannot be the priority that first world nations and their citizens seem to assume it to be.

In the second chapter, we hear the voices of those historically oppressed by Europeans and by those of European descent who conquered, colonized, and enslaved Africans and indigenous peoples in the Western Hemisphere since the Renaissance. Possibly our blindness to the effects of climate crisis on the poorest directly continue our unconsciousness of the radical injustices of colonialism and slavery, so rarely mentioned as sources of the very freedoms we enjoy, or of our material comforts. Not speaking or reading Spanish, many of us cannot hear the voices of the poor south of the Rio Grande, nor those of their prophets. Unwilling to recognize ourselves as beneficiaries of centuries of chattel slavery, we continue to imagine ourselves superior to the slaves' grandchildren. Our indigenous peoples are nearly invisible to most of us, except as curiosities. We call them "Native Americans," a term most of them despise. No wonder, living on so much deeply rooted and largely unconscious injustice, we cannot wake up to climate crisis as more than an inconvenience, perhaps even as a threat to our predictable ways of life. Not only have we inherited Enlightenment egoism in all its forms; we have been handed a sense of entitlement to land, dominance, and the nearly uncompensated labor of human beings we cannot see. Unconsciousness entitlement, historically unknown to us, keeps us blind to climate injustice as racism. When psychoanalysts, especially contemporary relational psychoanalysts, meet unconsciousness, they tend to bring it into dialogue.

The third chapter examines, less than exhaustively, some psychoanalytic resources for understanding, not so much the climate denial in political life, but rather the bystandership among us who do and do not know what is happening, just as we did and did not know about psychologists' heavy involvement in the US torture program. We consider the problems of shame and envy as they contribute to compulsive consumerism and ethical blindness. Finally, we make some practical suggestions for organized psychoanalysis if it wants to assume some ethical leadership in the climate emergency.

In the fourth and final chapter, we look for an ethical point of view adequate to wake us up to our personal and communal responsibilities. We acknowledge the valuable contributions of duty ethics, of utilitarianism, of deep ecology, but find that none of them suffices to create the needed sense of urgency. To move personal, communal, and political change in time to turn the tide in time to keep our earth, air, and oceans livable, we need an ethic that radically changes our way of seeing. We need to see the naked faces of those suffering and dying from our carbon-drunk way of life, to make the links, to see their vulnerability as our responsibility, one we cannot pass on to others. This final chapter argues that even though such an ethic is frankly anthropocentric in its motivation, its effects will heal our burning, broken earth, save many species, and teach us how to feed the hungry. It comes to much the same conclusions reached by the climate justice theorists considered in the first chapter.

I never wanted to write this book. It felt demanded, a responsibility from which I could not turn away, an urgent call. Somehow, this urgency, this "stop now!" forced this task upon me. At this point in life, beginning retirement from clinical practice, hoping to slow down, I would have wanted to write something reflective, even more literary. Hans-Georg Gadamer and R. E. Palmer (2007) distinguished between eminent artistic texts where one speaks of "a work" and those writings intended to be of service, more like handicraft. Unfortunately, the looming threat to our common home, and to its most vulnerable members, felt too demanding to proceed at leisure. Literary aspirations must wait. Literary or no, however, I must remind my readers and myself, that many better-prepared observers of our climate emergency, from many disciplines, are writing in this area. One more voice is only one more voice, and one more set of questions, challenges, and perspectives. I hope that others will join, if only to call out my errors.

But small and fallible as this book is, it needed the support of others: Kate Hawes, my acquisitions editor at Routledge, who said yes the moment I suggested it; colleagues who read drafts (Doris Brothers, Ali Crosthwait, Roger Frie, Lynne Jacobs, Steve Stern, Bob Stolorow) and helped me make the work coherent, my Pilgrim Place eco-intentional community here in Claremont, California, who surely inspired the project and mediated the call, wherever it came from. Here both communal and personal downsizing for the sake of justice and environmental responsibility, as well as many forms of political activism, characterize so-called retirement. An ethic of practical care for each other underlies this whole small world. Many of the elders here have suffered persecution for justice's sake, and to these pilgrimage companions I dedicate this small book. Most of all, as usual, my dear husband and meticulous editor Don Braue has read and studied every word, and made priceless suggestions. He generously lives out the radical ethics when I could not otherwise go on.

Many others, too, in writing and example, have helped me to feel this crisis and its effects on precarious lives. If I have not named you somewhere in this book, please accept my gratitude.

References

Freeman, M. (2012). The Narrative Unconscious. *Contemporary Psychoanalysis, 48,* 344–366.

Gadamer, H.-G., & Palmer, R. E. (2007). *The Gadamer reader: A bouquet of the later writings.* Evanston, IL: Northwestern University Press.

Grosskurth, P. (1986). *Melanie Klein: Her world and her work.* New York: Knopf.

McKibben, B. (2015, August 13). The Pope and the Planet. *The New York Review of Books, 62,* 40–42.

Orange, D. M. (1995). *Emotional understanding: studies in psychoanalytic epistemology.* New York: Guilford Press.

Orange, D. M. (2010). *Thinking for clinicians: Philosophical resources for contemporary psychoanalysis and the humanistic psychotherapies.* New York: Routledge.

Orange, D. M. (2011). *The suffering stranger: Hermeneutics for everyday clinical practice.* New York: Routledge.

Orange, D. (2016). *Nourishing the inner life of clinicians and humanitarians: The ethical turn in psychoanalysis.* London; New York: Routledge.

Young-Bruehl, E. (2008). *Anna Freud: A biography.* New Haven, CT: Yale University Press.

Chapter 1

Climate injustice and business as usual
What's wrong with this picture?

Cursed be the earth because of you.

(Genesis 3:17)

Perhaps many psychoanalysts know the climate crisis better than I have done until recently. As a young backpacker, I came to love the forests, streams, and mountains of the Pacific Northwest, and to feel strip mining and clearcutting forestry as travesties. But I saw environmental devastation as something other people committed, and kept trekking, no, driving innocently along through life. Even when Al Gore worked so hard just after the century's turn to convince us of the "inconvenient truth," his message didn't really penetrate or change the lives of many of us who spend our lives working with unconsciousness. Now it is nearly too late, and we must listen at our peril. But we listen backward: not only analyzing the unconsciousness: splitting, disavowal, melancholia (Lertzman, 2015), but also as in the biblical saying, and unlike most psychoanalysis, we reverse the listening sequence: "We will do, and we will hear," in that order. This chapter begins to explain what we need to learn scientifically and to consider psychoanalytically, even while we start to act ethically. Justice allows us no time to evade at psychoanalytic conferences—where we meet in luxurious hotels in cities full of homeless people—or to theorize at leisure. Our brothers and sisters are starving, drowning and burning while we dispute. But 60 million refugees in the year 2015, together with tornadoes and floods, may reset the alarm clock.

The science: what we have come to "know"

Emergency situations require immediate response. With ever-increasing intensity, climate scientists (IEA, 2015; IPCC, 2014a; NOAA, 2015) warn us that the warming of our oceans and atmosphere is increasing far faster than they had predicted even 5 or 10 years ago, and that we will probably reach very soon, and may have already reached, "tipping points" at which the damage to the earth and its biological inhabitants will be not only irreversible, but unmanageable. NOAA (National Oceanic and Atmospheric Administration) reports that July 2015 was the hottest month on record, 2015 the hottest year. The summer ice cap has nearly disappeared from the Arctic, while the West Antarctic ice sheet is slipping into the ocean. More and more species are already becoming extinct at a rate more than 100 times the "background rate," reports Paul Ehrlich of the Stanford Woods Institute for the Environment (Knapton, 2015), while human life rapidly degenerates into the "war of all against all" announced by philosopher Thomas Hobbes (Hobbes, Gaskin, & NetLibrary Inc., 1998) in the 18th century. Extremes of economic inequality—evident both within the USA and worldwide—though some consider them a separate problem—cannot, many of us believe, be addressed apart from the climate emergency. This chapter concerns the ways social justice and climate change intricately intertwine to form the question of climate justice.

First, the overwhelming majority of scientists agree that climate damage is largely self-inflicted, that is, that our addiction to fossil fuels and red meat is filling our atmosphere with toxic carbons and methane (www3.epa.gov/climatechange/ghgemissions/gases/ch4.html), melting the polar ice, and making ever-larger portions of our planet home into uninhabitable desert. The IPCC (International Panel on Climate Change) summary statement quoted below states clearly the current scientific consensus view of anthropogenic (human-caused) global warming and its consequences. Two new papers, one lead-authored by dean of climate scientists James Hansen[1] (Hansen et al., 2015), appeared while I was preparing this chapter, announcing that the polar ice is melting much faster than anyone had suspected. Threatening many northern species, this development means an emergency for whole peoples living near sea-level, needing relocation. Should they, by extraordinary good fortune, find hospitality, they will still have lost home, culture, and language.

I am no climate scientist, but am reading these scientific analysts of our shared situation as well as some of their clearest interpreters, modern-day prophets like Bill McKibben (McKibben, 2010, 2014), Vandana Shiva (Shiva, 2008), Naomi Klein (Klein, 2014), and most recently, Pope Francis (Catholic Church, 2015). McKibben, currently a leading voice in the movement toward disinvestment in fossil fuels and against the Keystone pipeline, can be contacted via his 350.org website. The "350" refers to carbon parts per million to which scientists say we should reduce carbon in the atmosphere to keep our planet livable. Vandana Shiva (Shiva, 2005, 2008, 2010), a quantum physicist who has given her life to promoting local and sustainable forms of agriculture, and fighting GMOs (genetically modified organisms), writes in her recent *Soil not Oil: Environmental Justice in an Age of Climate Crisis* (Shiva, 2008) that sustainable agriculture can save the poorest from the ravages of carbon. Probably her voice most moved me to write this book, and kept me at it. Find her at seedfreedom. info. Naomi Klein argues in great detail that most of us have avoided this "inconvenient truth" (Gore & Melcher Media, 2006) so long that now only an effort equivalent to that required to fight World War II, including enormous communal sacrifices like immediate conversion for a world without fossil fuels and rationing, will now save our planet with any shred of justice for those suffering most from the world created by industrialization and globalization. Unfortunately, no obvious enemy is dropping carbon bombs on our centers of commerce and culture, concentrating our minds. (Boswell [Boswell & Chapman, 2008] quotes Samuel Johnson: "When a man knows he is to be hanged . . . it concentrates his mind wonderfully." Sept. 19, 1777.)

Now Pope Francis has just published *Laudato Si*, "On the care for our common home," an encyclical linking the climate crisis to social justice. Despite his resounding silence on injustice toward women, inside and beyond the church, he directly focuses on the way climate change is devastating the world's poorest. These voices, and others, call us to repent, and quickly to change our ways. They appeal not to a punishing deity, but to the clear karmic (see also "The Time Is Now: Buddhist Declaration on Climate Change," 2015) consequences for our children and grandchildren if we do not act quickly.

In late 2014 one group of the world's most respected climate scientists, those who work together as the Intergovernmental Panel on Climate Change (IPCC, www.ipcc.ch/), told us what has already occurred. I quote at length to make sure I neither distort nor exaggerate the current situation nor the emergency we face:

> *Warming of the climate system is unequivocal, and since the 1950s, many of the observed changes are unprecedented over decades to millennia. The atmosphere and ocean have warmed, the amounts of snow and ice have diminished, and sea level has risen.*
>
> *Anthropogenic greenhouse gas emissions have increased since the pre-industrial era, driven largely by economic and population growth, and are now higher than ever. This has led to atmospheric concentrations of carbon dioxide, methane and nitrous oxide that are unprecedented in at least the last 800,000 years. Their effects, together with those of other anthropogenic drivers, have been detected throughout the climate system and are extremely likely to have been the dominant cause of the observed warming since the mid-20th century.*
>
> *In recent decades, changes in climate have caused impacts on natural and human systems on all continents and across the oceans. Impacts are due to observed climate change, irrespective of its cause, indicating the sensitivity of natural and human systems to changing climate.*
>
> *Changes in many extreme weather and climate events have been observed since about 1950. Some of these changes have been linked to human influences, including a decrease in cold temperature extremes, an increase in warm temperature extremes, an increase in extreme high sea levels and an increase in the number of heavy precipitation events in a number of regions.*
>
> (IPCC, 2014c)

The IPCC goes on to predict, based on multiple modeling, the foreseeable future, whether we do or do not make radical changes in the way we are living. They assume that significant "mitigation," that is, beginning to bring down our carbon usage to a 2 degree Centigrade atmospheric warming in this century, could keep the damage within adaptable limits. Continuing more or less on our current path will bring 4 degrees of warming, they warn, and defeat all possibility of adaptation to the conditions that will result (IPCC, 2014b).

> *Cumulative emissions of carbon dioxide largely determine global mean surface warming by the late 21st century and beyond. Projections of greenhouse gas emissions vary over a wide range, depending on both socio-economic development and climate policy. Surface temperature is projected to rise over the 21st century under all assessed emission scenarios.*
>
> *It is very likely that heat waves will occur more often and last longer, and that extreme precipitation events will become more intense and frequent in many regions. The ocean will continue to warm and acidify, and global mean sea level to rise. Climate change will amplify existing risks and create new risks for natural and human systems.*
>
> *Risks are unevenly distributed and are generally greater for disadvantaged people and communities in countries at all levels of development.*
>
> *Many aspects of climate change and associated impacts will continue for centuries, even if anthropogenic emissions of greenhouse gases are stopped. The risks of abrupt or irreversible changes increase as the magnitude of the warming increases.*
>
> (IPCC, 2014c, emphasis mine)

Many observers consider this alarming account, so carefully worded, based on the 2 and 4% Centigrade warming, as too conservative. A 2% goal, reachable only if we stop putting carbon into the atmosphere almost immediately, converting to renewable sources of energy by 2030, still leaves us on a path to irreversible damage requiring major adaptations. Even these moderate prognosticators explain that gradual warming will surely accumulate its effects, reaching "tipping points" after which the effects will aggregate more quickly and more catastrophically, leaving us little or no time to adapt, and none to reverse our course. Some observers (350.org, for example) say that we need to work for much less than 2% to protect the world's poorest from further desertification and sea level rise. James Hansen (J. Hansen, 2005; J. E. Hansen, 2009) has long argued that the 2% goal, agreed upon for mainly political reasons, is highly dangerous. Doing nothing about carbon means at least a 4% warming before the end of this century, with extremely probable catastrophic effects:

- **Heatwaves** of magnitudes never experienced before—temperatures not seen on Earth in the past five million years. Four degrees is only the average, so temperatures over large land masses will rise far higher.
- Forty percent of plant and animal species will be at risk of **extinction**.
- Precipitous **decline in the growth of crops** world wide, exacerbated by drought, floods and increased weed and pest invasion.
- Total melting of the Greenland ice sheet and, most likely, the Western Antarctic ice sheet **raising sea levels by thirty-two or more feet**—this would put two thirds of the world's major cities under water, as well as large regions of countries.
- **Once four degrees is reached there's no guarantee that temperatures would level off.**
- A population of nine billion will not be able to adapt to these conditions.

(www.climatepsychologyalliance.org/, adapted from Marshall, 2014)

Here we already see the implications of climate crisis for social justice, the major focus of Pope Francis's encyclical. Meanwhile, the more conservative but still very worried IPCC concludes, even under optimal conditions of mitigation, that is, radical reductions in carbon (from transport and all forms of energy production) and methane (mostly from fracking and livestock raising) emissions, limiting warming to 2 degrees Centigrade, significant climate changes already underway will require major adaptations, especially to protect the most vulnerable people. Whole island populations must relocate in the face of rising sea levels, while refugees from war and famine are already pouring into Europe (Ryde, in press). Without radical changes away from fossil fuels, including substantial decreases in consumption, initiated immediately, warming of 4 degrees is both extremely probable, they emphasize, and will make our planet uninhabitable by the end of this century. Like the IEA (International Energy Agency), the IPCC warns that every level (world, regional, national, sub-national, local) must make radical changes immediately to avoid the direst consequences.

They also tell us that the changes are still possible—including a complete change from fossil fuels by 2030—but will require vast mobilization of the world's richest countries, those who have contributed most to the problem. (Again, while I am writing, the Obama administration has announced the strongest regulations to limit coal-fired power plants to date. Although these fall far short of what is needed, massive opposition from established "energy" interests is organizing to defeat even this modest initiative.)

Yet most of us go on just as if we had not heard these warnings. Are our brains simply wired to exclude bad news, as George Marshall believes (Marshall, 2014), are we in the grip of "environmental melancholia" as social scientist reader of psychoanalysis Renee Lertzman (2015) thinks, or have we inherited a philosophical egoism, wedded to a narcissistic mindset full of entitlement, perhaps even of unconscious racist privilege inherited from millennia of slavery (Davis, 2006), the topic of Chapter 2, trapping and immobilizing us? All may be true, but if the disciplines of philosophy and psychoanalysis can help us to identify our problem quickly, then perhaps alliance with the world's moral and religious leaders can begin to shift the political tide, to create a "tipping point" of solidarity to meet the carbon tipping points already looming.

Enlightenment egoism

We Westerners inherit an outsized share of the guilt and responsibility for climate change. Whatever we may think of China now, we in the West set the industrialization-at-all-costs pattern it has followed. As Stephen M. Gardiner writes, "the USA is responsible for 29 percent of global emissions since the onset of the industrial revolutions (from 1850 to 2003), and the nations of the EU 26 percent; by contrast China and India are responsible for 8 percent and 2 percent respectively" (2011, p. 315). To understand what has gone so wrong in our relation to the earth, including our indifference to its most destitute people, we must first briefly revisit the roots of the scientific rationalism and political individualism emergent in 17th- and 18th-century Europe. These became founding ideals in the United States.

For many continental philosophers, Descartes (1596–1650), with his isolated-mind concept of the human as solitary substance, epitomizes our problem, originating the radical split between mind and nature, the human and the material world. He instituted the hegemony of mathematical reason, setting in motion our Western devotion to efficiency, technology, and statistics. Imagining that he achieved this feat himself, he taught us to think non-dialogically,[2] as well as in a manner that divorces reason from emotion and sensibility to the human and earthly environment.

More important, however, Galileo (1564–1642), the older contemporary whose bitter experience taught Descartes to be careful with religious authorities, became the father of modern science and technology. An astute observer of nature who noticed that pendula with larger and smaller arcs took the same time to swing, he moved to designing controlled experiments. But only in a vacuum do the heavy ball and the feather fall at the same rate. He had learned to isolate phenomena from their natural contexts, to control them, and then to regard as their true nature what he would then measure. He gave us the modern scientific method, with all the resources to control and dominate nature. And yet, he remains a hero to those of us who resent authoritarian religion. Ironically, we remember that the cardinals would not look through his telescope just as our fundamentalist contemporaries refuse to hear climate science. The story of Galileo reminds us that science has both brought us to the climate crisis, and for the most part, is now serving as prophetic voice to turn us back to the care of the natural world that science once taught us only to manipulate.

Many, however, would draw a straight line from the ancient Greeks to our current problems. Too much faith in rationality,[3] too much looking for totalizing, single explanations. All is one, said Parmenides, with Spinoza, Hegel, and Jung after him, not to mention the totalitarians (Arendt, 1951). But we have other options. Non-Western religion and philosophy offer many paths, while Western philosophy has additionally, from the time of Plato, developed dialogical approaches to truth-seeking, those leaving the conversation always open, always wanting to learn and understand more about the matter in question, seeing scientific rationality as only one path to the human, ever needing questioning and enrichment from the humanities. As a fundamental attitude, such dialogic thinking, such science pursued in a community of scholars always questioning its own premises, assumes that thinking belongs to the human community, not to the individual. It seeks common understanding, without closing off the road of inquiry, as pragmatist Charles Sanders Pierce would have said.

Fellow pragmatist William James articulated another alternative to the monistic presumptions of many philosophers, Western and Eastern alike. Calling his view pluralism, illustrating it best, I believe, in *The Varieties of Religious Experience* (James, 1902, 1977), James showed how rich and variegated is our access to whatever we feel and believe transcends us. Contemporary psychoanalysis, full of many voices, may also help us develop a concern beyond the autonomous ego of the glory days, a new sensitivity to the vulnerable earth, to its many precarious inhabitants, and to the suffering caused by our "culture of narcissism" (Lasch, 1978).

So although monism (it all comes down to the same thing) and egoism (it all comes out best if we care only for ourselves) have predominated in the so-called developed world, combining to form what Adriaan Peperzak calls "egocentric monism" (Peperzak & Levinas, 1993, p. 19), we have other possibilities.[4] Dialogic thinkers like Plato (Plato, Cooper, & Hutchinson, 1997), and Hans-Georg Gadamer (Gadamer & Palmer, 2007; Gadamer, Weinsheimer, & Marshall, 2004), pluralists like James (James, 1977), and ethical thinkers (Levinas, 1981) show that the West can value multiple voices, to whose prophetic call our final chapter returns.

Monism and climate crisis

Let us first consider monism as foundational to climate destruction. Monism, assuming the essential oneness of all things, further adopts, in its Western form, knowing or cognition as the exclusive—or at least primary—route or form of access to this one total reality. Hegel, probably the most capable practitioner of this approach, proclaimed:

> What human beings strive for in general is cognition of the world; we strive to appropriate it and to conquer it. To this end the world must be crushed as it were; i.e. it must be made ideal.
> (Hegel, Geraets, Suchting, & Harris, 1991, p. 85)

Merold Westphal (Westphal, 1998), to whom I am indebted for drawing my attention to these stunning words, comments that Hegel "let the cat out of the bag" about his totalizing intentions. A different cat interests me. Hegel tells us that our passion for knowing the world prepares us to treat the earth as our possession, "appropriate it," to dominate it (and its indigenous peoples?), that is, to "conquer it," and to crush it in the service of making it ideal, that is, a mental product. Not only Genesis, probably misunderstood, but also Enlightenment rationalism taught us to dominate by knowing, to crush, not to take care.

Thinking back, I remember being taught as a child to memorize the "natural resources" of the places we studied in geography class, including minerals, forests, sometimes fish and other animals. Now I realize that, from the viewpoint of the United States in the 1950s, we were meant to learn what could be extracted from these faraway countries, then often known by colonial names, to grow the economy here. The people in these places, considered exotic and "primitive," had nothing to teach us in our vast superiority. To study the world was to learn to dominate.

While a passion for knowing[5] may, instead, serve humanistic, ecological, and transcendent purposes—curing disease, alerting us to climate dangers, connecting us to others geographically distant and culturally strange to us—cognition as master rather than servant destroys, appropriating, dominating, and conquering, just as Hegel wrote. It destroys the hermeneutic space (Figal, 2010; Sassenfeld, 2016) where understanding emerges, creativity flourishes, indigenous cultures live, and individual, irreplaceable human beings (Levinas, 1969) must not be crushed. Hegemonic, all-dominating, scientific reason evokes Pascal's thought: "My place in the sun begins the destruction of the earth" (*C'est là ma place au soleil. Voilà le commencement et l'image de l'usurpation de toute la terre*) (Pascal & Levi, 2008, p. 25).

Pascal clearly links possessiveness to the destruction of the earth. Perhaps a clear-headed look at the climate crisis will require us to rethink our culture's deeply embedded assumptions about private property, consumption, and their associated "rights." (Many commentators remarked during the recent Paris talks that carbon pollution knows no national borders.) New questions arise, for governments and also for individuals. May I keep watering my lawn when others in my state have no drinking water and vast areas are burning out of control every year? May I keep drinking a bottle of wine or two bottles of beer each evening without asking myself how much water it takes to produce these pleasures, or whether, perhaps, they can be sustainably produced? May I own five homes, or even one mansion, when many in the world, even in my own city, have none? May I keep eating beef whose production fills the atmosphere with toxic methane gas? These are only a few of the pragmatic questions to be asked of an egoistic ethics of the absolute rights of private property. Not abstract philosophical questions, these concrete, urgent questions challenge each of us daily to say whether we will continue the complacent lifestyles that destroy our common home or start a serious transformation.

We return for the moment, however, to the roots of our slide into climate disaster. Early Enlightenment philosopher Thomas Hobbes described human life in the state of nature as "solitary, poor, nasty, brutish, and short" (Hobbes et al., 1998, p. 77). Egoism, he realized, was ugly. Against the divine right of kings, he believed society consisted in the forming of social contracts in which each individual agreed to yield some of "his" freedom to create a workable whole, and thus to limit the effects of the self-interest rampant in the state of nature. We form social contracts for our self-preservation. John Locke, the philosopher most read by the writers of the U.S. Declaration of Independence and Constitution, agreed and developed social contract theory into a political philosophy (Locke, Shapiro, & Locke, 2003), in which the rights of individual property owners stood paramount. Governments, as limited as possible, exist to protect individual rights, especially rights to private property and freedom from the imposition of state religion. "All men are created equal," proclaims the beloved document; slaves, the spoils of war, were sub-human property. Unlike Hobbes, Locke accorded to women greater-than-property status, but they did not rise to equality as citizens.

Unsurprising, then, that such a philosophy[6] "entitled" its believers to colonial appropriation of the lands of indigenous peoples, to the destruction of their earth-loving ways of life, to slave-ownership and inheritance enforced by the lash, to the subjection of women. Egoism blinds us to the intrinsic value and dignity of whatever or whomever we dominate, reducing the "thou" (Buber & Kaufmann, 1970) to solely instrumental value, the "it." What we own, we may exploit, use and abuse, even destroy. With this philosophy firmly in our background, many in the United States—from where I write—can see no serious problem with our legacy of slavery,[7] with the continued subjection of the few remaining descendants of our native peoples, and with exploiting and destroying the earth that is our common home.[8] Much less can most of us truly feel connected to others in Latin America, Asia, and Africa being destroyed already by our way of life, and sometimes turning to jihad. Our philosophical and ethical unconsciousness, our profound individualistic egoism, prevents us from noticing both what we are doing to each other and to our planet as well as to the ways we are beneficiaries of the slave system, of colonialism, and of carbon-dependent industrialism. Unconsciousness blinds us to egoism's devastating consequences. We cannot see ourselves in the wrong. Our next chapter returns to this aspect of climate unconsciousness.

Individualistic egoism, in its many forms, severely limits our capacities to register and genuinely to confront the climate crisis. Phenomenologist Will Adams writes that it limits our attitudes toward nature: "(1) an objectified resource to exploit; (2) a dreaded threat; (3) an impediment to my self-centered projects; or (4) unnoticed and irrelevant" (Adams, 2015, p. 34). These attitudes toward nature closely relate to the concept of moral freedom philosopher Judith Butler describes:

> if we think moral authority is about finding one's will and standing by it, stamping one's name upon one's will, it may be that we miss the very mode by which moral demands are relayed. That is, we miss the situation of being addressed, the demand that comes from elsewhere, sometimes a nameless elsewhere by which our obligations are articulated and pressed upon us.
>
> (Butler, 2004, p. 130)

This moral individualism, hearing only one's own voice, needs, desires, and projects, noted by both Adams and Butler, lies, I believe, at the historical root of the climate crisis, and keeps it intractable.

By contrast, we may hear a demand to focus on this problem *now*. Butler goes on to explain:

> what is morally binding . . . does not proceed from my autonomy or my reflexivity. It comes to me from elsewhere, unbidden,

unexpected, and unplanned. In fact, it tends to ruin my plans, and if my plans are ruined, that may well be the sign that something is morally binding on me.

(Butler, 2004, p. 130)

Just as a family illness, a stranger falling on the street, or an earthquake in Haiti or Nepal may change my plans and demand my attention and response, so climate justice—once it genuinely penetrates the forms of unconsciousness we consider in our next chapter—becomes Butler's disruptor "from elsewhere," ruining my plans to go on comfortably as I have always lived, or to give myself a rest. Something is morally binding on me. In our final chapter we return to this form of responsibility, and consider whether it can help to mobilize us. Meanwhile, many of us have not yet heard climate crisis as a call "from elsewhere," as a cry for social justice.

So let us consider the impact of psychological trauma on our capacities to act, hear, and feel, in this crisis we are living. Recent psychoanalytic experience and theorizing can teach us something, perhaps.

Trauma and loss of solidarity

Even when the arrival of grandchildren begins to alarm us about their future, we remain in our "little boxes," recycling as we can, perhaps driving hybrid cars, but mostly concerned about our daily lives. A kind of double-mindedness develops: we know we should, even must, do something, but the problems seem so large and systemic, so intractable in the face of gigantic moneyed interests that control national and state politics, that we find ourselves paralyzed. Unwittingly, we find ourselves in the grip of climate trauma.

Here let me say just enough to begin thinking about the ways this crisis has hit us, what it means for us to realize that we can no longer plan for the future on the basis of the past, and so on. How are we traumatized by what we have done to the world we have treated as our disposable possession, wondering how we and our children must respond to what we have done? How do we respond to realizing how severely our most destitute sisters and brothers are traumatized, even destroyed? How do we each experience climate trauma, and how can we help each other emerge from its paralysis?

One need not be aware of it to be suffering from psychological trauma. Several years ago, having encountered a disturbing error message on my computer, I called technical support. The competent helper, whose accent I recognized as coming from India, managed in a half-hour or so to solve my problem. During a pause, when I asked where he was located, he named an area of southern India. "Were you close to the tsunami?" I asked. "Oh yes, but we are all safe here, and all my family too, some of whom were much more exposed. Thank you for asking." Then he began to repeat, almost singsong style, "It was so unexpected. We didn't expect it. It was so unexpected. We didn't expect it." We returned to our task, but as soon as there was another pause, the refrain returned. "It was so unexpected. We didn't expect it. Thank you for your concern. Thank you for asking," and so on. Even when our task was success-fully completed, it was difficult to end the call.

This incident[9] illustrates several aspects of the phenomenology of traumatic experience, familiar to all clinicians and humanitarian workers: the destruction of temporality, the violation of expectancy, emotional freezing, the need for witnessing, the selective disorgani-zation of experience, and mourning.

Trauma—whether natural disaster, human violence, or unexpected loss—destroys our normal sense of time (Stolorow, 2007). We lose the feeling that "I'll see you tomorrow" (*hasta la vista, arrivederci*) makes any sense. Organizing our lives toward a future, our own or that of those we love, loses sense. We feel dazed, disoriented, and lost. Trauma often destroys memory, both for the traumatic experi-ence itself, or for the life before and around it.

Trauma also creates emotional freezing, a deer-in-the-headlights experience. It may seem impossible to feel what is happening to us, or to respond appropriately, to move away from the path of the

Mack truck. Paralysis prevents action on behalf of ourselves or others. Here is another example, from historian Thomas Kohut:

> Some years ago, my family and I visited a friend and her daughter in Brussels in Belgium. . . . She comes from a Jewish family and survived the Holocaust, with her parents and siblings, by hiding in Brussels. During our visit, we made a walking tour of the city and, turning a corner, came upon a small construction site in the sidewalk. There was a hole in the pavement, about a yard deep, with a wooden walkway over it and a railing. But when our Belgian friend saw this construction site, she cried out in a panicked voice, "Watch out! Be careful! It's dangerous!" In reality the construction site was not dangerous, not even for our children. But her reaction, her panic-stricken reaction, was so familiar to me. My father [Heinz Kohut] could have—would have—reacted in the same way. He too survived the Holocaust, fleeing Austria as a young man in 1939. And I must confess that I too have this panicky reaction at times. The world is bright and colorful, the sun is shining. But then out of the corner of the eye one glimpses a little spot of gray, and suddenly one is seized with a terrible anxiety that this little spot will suddenly cover the whole colorful scene in black. From our contemporary perspective, the source of this so exaggerated reaction is not difficult to identify. It was produced by the historical reality of the Holocaust. It happened once, exactly like that. The world was bright and colorful, the sun was shining. But suddenly one found oneself in the middle of a lethal situation. What today seems such an unrealistic and inappropriate panic was, back then, a realistic and appropriate reaction to a situation of extreme danger. The relatives of my father, his aunts and uncles who did not have his panic-stricken reaction and remained in Austria, were all exterminated.
>
> (T. Kohut, 2003, p. 225)

The parallel with our climate emergency is clear: when we cannot panic appropriately, we cannot take fittingly radical action.[10] (Recent examples of lives saved when tornado warnings are heeded, however, show that people can learn to respond when the threat becomes clear enough. Applying this lesson to climate crisis becomes a massive and urgent task for educators and governments.)

Trauma violates expectancy. Whatever we previously took for granted: the presence of our loved ones, our own health, the ground under our feet (I currently live 15 miles from the San Andreas Fault), even the likelihood of a future, all this is gone. All is confusion and nothing is reliable. We cannot, expectancies violated, believe the evidence of our own eyes. One of my neighbors recently protested repeatedly that a tall tree near her house was brown on its top this year. Come and look, she insisted, come and look, as if the local tree expert could change this. That many trees in Claremont, California, look this way after four years of severe drought could not be believed, could not be assimilated into her reality. She was in shock.

In trauma we may also suffer a shocking narcissistic injury, that is, a painful blow to our sense of self, of entitlement, of our place in the universe. Freud told us that his discovery of the unconscious— though some would dispute his claim to having discovered this— was such a shocking blow. We are no longer masters in our own house, he said. Neither are we. Of course, we never were. We were guests, and perhaps stewards, but thought we were lords, masters, and owners. The climate crisis teaches painful and long-needed lessons in humility, lessons that most of us do not receive with gratitude. For years we have been like students who read the book about our probable, now almost certain, future, and replaced it on the shelf.

The climate crisis, once grasped, traumatizes in all these ways. It forces us to revalue our past and to doubt our future. Not only will any future differ from the past in ways we would not have foreseen, it will differ in ways no one could possibly want. For many there will be no future, for others there will be terrible suffering, the consequence of the developed world's mindless self-absorption. The "good old days" are becoming a well of guilt, inducing further emotional paralysis.

Emotional freezing[11] takes several forms: splitting what we now *can* see from our sense of responsibility (popularly called compart-mentalizing), throwing up our hands, loss of solidarity. Those floods,

fires, earthquakes caused by oil drilling and fracking, polar ice melting, are elsewhere, in Alaska, Africa, Asian islands, somewhere else,
perhaps even in a different district within my own city. My world,
thank God—what a blasphemy—is still all right. I can worry about
which car I should buy next, getting my children into the best col-
leges, finding the best restaurant for Saturday night. The same self-
centeredness, the me-first, more-is-better economics that created the
climate crisis, paralyzes our possibilities for creative coping.

Violation of expectancies disorients everyone. The earth we
believed was our home and our mother can now seem to be our
enemy. And yet, such violations, whether arriving as climate events
or economic events, can occasion either further paralysis or creative
response.

Unequal trauma

We must also acknowledge that the climate crisis affects us humans
unequally, that some of us are still reasonably comfortable while
many, and increasingly a large majority, are hungry and destitute.
Some of us have far more coping resources than do our brothers
and sisters across the tracks or across the world. We might say with
Emmanuel Levinas, phenomenologist and prophet whose radical
ethics we take up later, that to respond ethically, we must allow
ourselves to be traumatized, taken hostage by the useless suffering
of these others. From the Talmud he quoted: "To leave men without food is a fault that no circumstance attenuates; the distinction
between the voluntary and the involuntary does not apply here"
(Levinas, 1979, p. 201). In other words, not knowing that my lifestyle creates starvation and misery for others is no excuse; the fault
remains. (Thus, climate justice theorists speak of "carbon debt" that
polluters like us owe to those whose health and survival continues to
be destroyed by our way of life, whether we know it or not.) Levinas
commented: "Before the hunger of men, responsibility is measured
only 'objectively;' it is irrecusable" (p. 201). He often quoted from
Dostoevsky's *Brothers Karamazov*, "We are guilty/responsible of all

and before all, and I more than all the others." Double-mindedness, even when traumatically induced, does not exonerate but simply leads to "we didn't know anything" from people who saw their neighbors loaded into boxcars and taken away. We too are pretending to ourselves not to know, especially how our lives of privilege impoverish and endanger our fellow human beings.

But traumatically paralyzed, we may not notice our guilt and responsibility. Or we may feel so overwhelmed by the outsized proportions of this crisis that we cannot imagine where to begin, and find ourselves just going on as before. Robert Stolorow (2013) speculates about the resulting avoidance:

> An explanation of the evasion perhaps requires a shift from a philosophical to a psychoanalytic perspective emphasizing the unbearable emotions that would accompany a facing-up to a doomsday scenario with its collapse of meaning. It is from the *horror* of the doomsday scenario posed by climate change that the minimizers, scoffers, and ridiculers turn away. Ironically, in turning away from the extreme dangers of climate change, we contribute to the coming to be of the horrifying catastrophe we are evading. We must face up to our apocalyptic anxiety before it is too late for the survival of future generations. Such facing-up requires that we open a far-reaching emotional dialogue in which the *Angst* can be collectively held and borne.

He is surely right, but how are we to organize a "far-reaching emotional dialogue" in such a short time? "The fierce urgency of now" (King, 1963) worries many of us: by the time we wake up, millions more of the world's poorest will have died from hunger, and global warming's worst effects may be irremediable. We will need the holding dialogue in any case, to help us mourn while bearing anxieties that otherwise paralyze us.

A small sidebar here: we may worry that climate responsibility requires us to prioritize the needs of the earth over those of people. This problem appears in two forms: (1) what I call ecological romanticism, and (2) ecoengineering proposals. The first has many forms. It may escape catastrophe into dreams and fantasies of returning to the beautiful earth of once-upon-a-time, and need not preoccupy us here. (As escapism, it prevents action; as reverence, combined with a serious account of where we actually are, however, it may help some to sustain action.) Romanticism also reappears in "deep ecology," the environmentalism of many serious people, a view I take up in Chapter 4. The second, more dangerous, ecoengineering fantasy believes that billionaires will invent a technological fix for our climate crisis, so that the rest of us, including politicians, need do nothing. Some propose extracting carbon from the atmosphere as part of meeting decarbonizing targets, as if we already had the technology to do this, and knew what the side-effects would be. Some even imagine an escape to other planets for those rich enough to afford it. These solutions, at least those proposed until now, mostly advantage those already advantaged, releasing them from any obligation to change their carbon-and-methane profligate consumerist lifestyles, and abandon the Southern Hemisphere (Klein, 2014). This form of climate concern consists in magical thinking (Ogden, 2010), absolving us from all responsibility. Once we realize, instead, that earth protection can result precisely from care for the poorest and most destitute, just as Vandana Shiva (2008) argues, the ethical problem, earth versus people, disappears. Nations like Venezuela and Mexico, for example, whose economies depend substantially on oil production and trading, need substantial investment from outside in green energy if decarbonizing is not to increase the already terrible numbers and suffering of their poorest people. When we ask what the most destitute need to live with dignity, the answers usually concern water and access to environmentally friendly energy sources so that they can grow their own food and their own small enterprises.

Mourning and repentance

Psychoanalysts speak of the necessity to mourn our losses of significant figures if we are to integrate the best of what they have been to us into our own personalities (Loewald, 1962, 1973, 1988). We often speak of mourning traumatic losses, witnessed by the community, or if necessary by the analyst, so that anything possible may be retrieved for internalization, even when it seems that all has been destroyed. Often the most difficult emotional work involves terrible shame over the ways in which we patients—and we are all patients, sooner or later—have contributed to our own destruction. In the process of witnessed mourning, new relational possibilities sometimes emerge, and create partial healing of the previously unbearable wounds. (Shame, however, as we will see in considering its most pervasive forms [Chapter 3], can also hide climate crisis from us almost completely.) Otherwise the ghosts of the unconscious, of whom we will have more to say, continue to haunt our traumatized souls, preventing us from seeing the faces of those suffering from our mindless consumerism.

Does this mourning-and-internalization story help us with the traumatic realization and impact of the climate emergency? I would guess that we need at least one additional element, borrowed from several of the world's religions: repentance. In a recent opinion piece, a native of Los Angeles recalled in detail how he personally had contributed to the climate crisis by driving everywhere mindlessly. Even now, much more thoughtful, he flies for work regularly. Similarly, I may stop eating beef and replace it with yogurt and cottage cheese, forgetting that all three come from the cattle spewing methane into the atmosphere, creating global warming many times faster than carbon emissions do.

Calling ourselves out, accusing ourselves of our sins against our earth, our fellow species, and against each other, will humble us, force us to mourn, and help us to undertake a new path, pointed out to us by each other. In this humbler spirit, no one will claim to know the way, but all will search together and speak by listening, especially to the voices of our indigenous peoples who knew and know how to live close to the earth. We can unpretentiously take up our call to be each other's keeper, and in the process, begin to heal our wounded earth.

Toward climate justice

We have not yet defined the term "climate justice." It involves, I think, two inextricable elements: (1) reducing carbon in the atmosphere to the 350 parts per million needed for a livable planet (NASA, 2008), and (2) doing this in a way that not only does not further harm the world's most vulnerable people, but also restores some measure of basic dignity to their lives. Implicitly this definition claims that climate justice is restorative justice, that the rich of the world must come to see ourselves as having perpetrated, and continuing to perpetrate, massive injustice against the world's poorest, and see ourselves as owing restitution. (The recent Paris talks make it clear that restorative justice is a hard sell in the Global North.) Other definitions improve on mine, but the best ones include these two essentials.

Justice comes in various forms. John Rawls (1971) formulated *distributive justice* while Thomas Pogge has extended it globally to address unjustifiable and gross economic inequalities and inequities. *Procedural justice* concerns the rights of parties to be heard, personally, or at the international table. Parity, or *participatory justice*, for voices of indigenous peoples who may not have national governments in the UN sense, often arises here. Participatory parity, according to Figueroa (Figueroa, 2011), "in adaptation and mitigation would resemble the Nunavik Research Centre, an organization that responds to climate change, whose strategies include involving indigenous residents, non-indigenous scientists, participatory research, a method for addressing issues raised by residents, and checks along the process that are reviewed by elders" (p. 237). *Recognition justice* comes in to make claims about who counts as claiming a voice or as having suffered damage. Questions of civil rights, and of human rights generally, for example, the rights not to have one's body attacked or invaded without one's consent, arise here. *Restorative justice* (Gobodo-Madikizela, 2016) usually attempts repair and restitution for wrongs committed, especially by means of participation by victims, perpetrators, and bystanders. It involves witnessing beyond recognition questions, and often includes perpetrators who may not have known they were doing these wrongs. Such restorative justice will return, at least implicitly, in our discussions of chattel slavery and settler colonialism. *Intergenerational justice* points to obligations we have to those not yet born, who may rightly accuse of us of having destroyed the nest by our mindless and profligate lives. Recently, Henry Shue (2014) has formulated a conception of "background injustice" to which we return in Chapter 2. All these concepts form parts of what we commonly call "social justice," a much larger question than the distributive justice with which it is sometimes simply equated, as well as of the climate justice we address here.

Any workable definition of climate justice stands on a basic assumption, clearly stated in the recent encyclical: "We are faced not with two separate crises, one environmental and the other social, but rather with one complex crisis which is both social and environmental. Strategies for a solution demand an integrated approach to combating poverty, restoring dignity to the excluded, and at the same time protecting nature" (#139). We must severely limit carbon emissions while protecting and restoring the lives of the most fragile people. *Without justice for the poor, why save the planet?*

More insistently and yet more carefully and fallibilistically (always prepared to revise his earlier opinions) than most, Henry Shue (Shue, 2014), though joined by many others (Gardiner, 2010; Jamieson, 2003, 2014; Klein, 2014), has long advocated in international circles for policies to address climate change that simultaneously tackle climate injustice. Solutions he once thought reasonable have become impossible now, after the worst polluters have been unwilling to make significant changes for so long, warming continues to worsen, and its effects accumulate (I was going to say snowball, a bad metaphor here). Carbon taxes, unless exempting the poorest, create more misery, making it impossible for many to exist at a subsistence level. Like Pope Francis, Shue opposes cap-and-trade proposals because they do not reduce emissions and induce magical thinking, in which emissions go away or become less harmful if we pay for them. Instead, as so many have remarked that it has become a commonplace, cap-and-trade resembles a system for selling indulgences, so that the richest can go on sinning. The poorest have nothing to trade, another aspect that we may systematically not notice, adding to our ethical unconsciousness. Shue notes that both carbon taxes, attempting to affect behavior with higher prices, and cap-and-trade schemes, further harm the poor by raising prices and preventing their bare subsistence. With Mary Robinson and a group of other ethicists, Shue has given us the clearest statement of principles (see Appendix 1) that I know, against which all mitigation and adaptation proposals must be measured. The option to do nothing we cannot consider.

And yet, writes Shue, there is good news on the climate justice front:

> We have two strong negative duties: a duty not to continue to undermine the climate, which would make life much more difficult for everyone in generations somewhat farther into the future, and a duty not to increase the obstacles to development for the current poor and their immediate successors. The two duties are additive, but the beauty of fulfilling them by developing affordable, renewable energy is that such measures would fulfill both at once.
>
> (Shue, 2014, p. 337)

Best of all, the climate justice movement, led by Mary Robinson (2015), has strongly embraced the new papal encyclical's approach as identical to its own, reaffirming in the clearest possible terms that *the climate crisis is a crisis of social justice*, first and foremost. "There has been a growing conviction that our planet is our homeland and that humanity is one people living in a common home," writes Pope Francis, the first world leader to speak clearly and passionately to this crisis. Convinced, like all climate justice theorists and activists, that climate abuse and social injustice are inextricably linked, he has written a moral *tour de force*. One need not share his religious point of view, or his masculinist opinions; he appeals to all who share our "common home." Non-evasively, he confronts the powerful with their obligation: "Reducing greenhouse gas emissions requires honesty, courage and responsibility, above all on the part of those countries which are more powerful and pollute the most." Using water as an example, he enunciates in one sentence both the principle of climate debt, and that of a fundamental human right: "Our world has a grave social debt towards the poor who lack access to drinking water, because they are denied the right to a life consistent with their inalienable dignity" (pp. 23–24).

Given our actual situation in 2016, what could climate justice look like? Granted, some argue that extreme problems require us to disregard many voices, and to choose the most efficient means to make change immediately. Not only do I find this thinking ethically problematic, but I suspect that without local-level investment and participatory democracy, any solutions will turn out short-lived, fragile, and authoritarian. They will perpetrate injustice in the name of survival. (We might note that, while demanding that urban California reduce water usage by certain percentages, Governor Jerry Brown has left it to local governments to devise the methods. As of this writing, the response has exceeded his targets.) So apart from *Besserwisser* (knowing-better, know it all) answers that tell local communities what they need, what else must we urgently consider?

Tikkun,[12] under the leadership of Rabbi Michael Lerner, advocates a domestic and global Marshall Plan, including ESRA (The Environmental and Social Responsibility Amendment) to the U.S. Constitution (www.tikkun.org/nextgen/a-real-solution-to-environmental-sustainability). It would include (1) undoing *Citizens United*,[13] and eliminating private money from all elections at every level; (2) re-chartering the largest corporations every five years according to strict social responsibility criteria; (3) teaching environmental responsibility and non-violent democracy in all schools; and (4) overturning all trade treaties with harmful environmental effects. The Domestic and Global Marshall Plan section would obligate the United States to convince the 20 richest countries of the world to give 1–2% of GDP to eliminate poverty and reverse environmental degradation caused by centuries of colonization and exploitation worldwide (tikkun.org/gmp).

We may note that this plan implies, though does not stipulate, immediate conversion from fossil fuels to wind and solar, as well as a massive turn away from industrialized agriculture and beef farming. It assumes that reducing the political power of the lobbies for coal, oil, shale, and industrial farming will ensure their quick reduction.

Whether or not all these assumptions work, I do not know, and leave to wiser political minds. I miss a clear description of the harm climate injustice is wreaking on the world's poor (though clearly *Tikkun* has exactly this in mind). Without specifics, talk of "inequality" and "injustice" become abstractions. Instead, let us compare the mega-mansions in the Hamptons and the $90 million apartments in New York, often owned by the same people, with the wretched, sub-human, housing of those still trying, years later, to recover from hurricanes Katrina and Sandy. Let us think of the severely impoverished lives of those who clean rooms and toilets in luxury hotels, as well as the wretched living and working conditions of those who make our clothes in faraway, unseen countries. Let us compare the wealth of fossil fuel billionaires with the impoverished refugees from the war-torn countries from which their (and our) oil comes. Let us remember that our economic security depends on the radical insecurity—Judith Butler calls it "precarity"—of the miserable lives of those we deem worthless worldwide but whose misery makes our comfort possible. Gill Straker (2004, 2011) calls us "beneficiaries" of the evil we refuse to see, but in which we mindlessly participate, as in apartheid South Africa.

Many interested in climate justice see the first step as providing renewable energy resources to the poorest people, so that they can grow their own economies, and renew traditional agricultural practices. Others add that radically reducing almost every kind of consumption in the developed world will be necessary to slow the rate of atmospheric warming—though I notice little mainstream interest in such downsizing of our lifestyles. Most important, *we must not untangle the needs of the poor from the climate question.* This seems the great ethical temptation, moral blindness.

To find a path toward climate justice would mean to see, really to see and feel, these injustices, in concrete ways. Building fences along our borders to keep refugees out so that we can continue to live in comfort means pretending that we have nothing to do with their misery. It means forgetting, in collective and personal unconsciousness, that our government massively supported the violent dictatorships whose corrupt successors these refugees we call "illegal aliens" are fleeing. It extends the absolutism of private property to the autocracy of national sovereignty, as "my country" meant exclusion, not "give me your tired, your poor, your huddled masses yearning to breathe free" that welcomed our grandparents here. These attitudes follow directly from the egoism discussed above, and have become so commonplace that we barely notice them, even if, on reflection, we would not agree.

But how many of us, psychoanalysts included, think of radically altering our way of life so that all can live humanly? So that all can breathe clean air, so that all can have uncontaminated water to drink, so that warming can be controlled so that desertification does not starve more millions of the world's children? Most of us have not even begun to imagine a way of life that would be more just, or the re-distribution that it would require. Not in my back yard—that windmill may spoil my view, let alone those solar panels or those refugees.[14] Rezoning so that more people could live in our oversized houses might threaten our property values. Bicycle and bus lanes might slow down single-passenger cars. Where is our moral imagination, or better, how can we develop it?

We do need leaders, prophets, and visionaries. On the protest and resistance side, we have Bill McKibben, fighting the Keystone pipeline, and pushing divestment in fossil fuels, even challenging Pope Francis to divest the Vatican. Others like Michael Lerner call for a Marshall Plan to make those who have grown rich from carbon pay restitution. Activists everywhere are taking to the streets and joining indigenous peoples to obstruct new and more dangerous extraction of fossil fuels.

But we also need to envision a future of climate justice, of human solidarity in harmony with the earth. Martin Luther King told us he had a dream, not only for racial equality and dignity, but for economic justice. I wonder what he would be saying now. What kind of world would John Lennon sing now that we might imagine to replace religious wars, and our preoccupation with maintaining world domination? What should be our dream of the post-carbon world, the world in which together we recover from its destructiveness while building a communal and creative future? It cannot be the "Dream" Ta-Nehisi Coates mocks in *Between the World and Me* (2015), a dream of white-picket fences excluding, even raping, everyone with darker skin. He challenges our moral imagination beyond such dreams, forcing us to see what havoc we have wreaked.

In practical terms, Vandana Shiva imagines a world without Monsanto controlling every seed put into the ground, and then into our bodies. She replaces industrialized agriculture with native, indigenous seeds and farming. Similarly, Wes Jackson imagines, and creates the possibility of, a sustainable agriculture of grains from perennial grasses and other drought-resistant food. Recently (June, 2015), nearly 2,000 thinkers and activists descended on Claremont, California, to hear the bad news and to consider what comes next in a conference named "Seizing an Alternative: Toward an Ecological Civilization."[15] Sandra Lubarsky, a section leader at this conference and professor of sustainable development at Appalachian State University, approaches the imagination question by considering hope and despair. Having advised us, in the gallows humor of Holocaust people, to save our despair for when we really need it, she advises us to seize on "radical hope." She defines such hope as:

> hope that is sustained not simply by sheer force of personal conviction or by willful ignorance of reality or because of a privileged immunity from reality's worst contingencies. Radical hope is secured—in its roots—by a metaphysics that affirms: change and possibility, agency and power, novelty and creativity, and value and importance.
>
> (www.pandopopulus.com/lubarsky-on-hope/#!)

Likewise, Tony Cartwright (www.climatepsychologyalliance.org/everything-and-nothing-radical-hope-in-a-time-of-climate-change/) appeals to Jonathan Lear's account, *Radical Hope: Ethics in the Face of Cultural Devastation* (Lear, 2006),[16] of Plenty Coups, the last great Crow chief who spoke:

> When the buffalo went away the hearts of my people fell to the ground and they could not lift them up again. After this nothing happened.

Philosopher/psychoanalyst Jonathan Lear considers at length what it means to say that nothing more happens after the world we know has been destroyed. In a communal existential trauma, the whole framework of concepts, the lifeworld, that gave daily life meaning, has disappeared, so that nothing happens in the sense it did before. All is a gray nothing. To go on means finding what Lear calls radical hope, "directed toward a future goodness that transcends the current ability to understand what it is" (p. 103). Plenty Coups advised the Crow to go to the white man's schools, and learn to adapt, to learn a new form of courage completely unlike the courage needed in the warrior life in the world with the buffalo. From devastation they had to find a new way, not pretending they could get the old life back. In his older years, Plenty Coups looked back:

> The Crows were wiser. We knew the white men were strong, without number in their country, and that there was no good fighting them; so that when other tribes wished us to fight them we refused. Our leading chiefs saw that to help the white men fight their enemies and ours would make them our friends. We had always fought the three tribes, Sioux, Cheyenne, and Arapahoe, anyway and might as well do so now. The complete destruction of our old enemies would please us. Our decision was reached, not because we loved the white man who was already crowding other tribes into our country, or because we hated the Sioux, Cheyenne, and Arapahoe, but because we plainly saw that this course was the only one which might save

our beautiful country for us. When I think back my heart sings because we acted as we did. It was the only way open for us.

(Linderman & Linderman, 1972, p. 85)

Whatever later generations of indigenous leaders may think of Plenty Coups's solution and reasoning (and this I do not know), we will need such wisdom, envisioning new forms of life in the aftermath of our consumerist culture, to sustain radical hope for any future during and after climate change. Actually, "during" and "after" make no sense in this strange temporality; thus we need a *radical* hope.

As a "we," we must find the ways open to us, ways we cannot yet see. Clearly we cannot revert to the individualism that has brought us to this crisis. All my life it has struck me as more than strange that people commonly identify a person's worth with the amount of money she or he possesses. "He is worth five million," we might say, while "she is worth only three." My identity depends on the dollars I possess, not on my network of relationships to people, buffalo, values, or anything else. What I possess is who I am. Radical hope, I think, will mean finding the courage to organize an alternative sense of personal meaning, unlinked to accumulating things, money, academic degrees, or power. Meaning will be linked, as in many indigenous communities, to the possibilities for sharing and reverence. Then I may possess little, but am never really impoverished. The infinite value psychoanalysts have always attached to the experience, suffering, and potential development of the irreplaceable human person may bring an insistently alternative voice to the urgent search for climate justice.

Assuming we can hope, not for the world of the past—the world of hierarchies of wealth, gender, race, and so on, a world of familiar comforts in which more is better—but for some kind of new world, how might we imagine it? Can we move beyond diagnosis to imagination in psychoanalysis? If we can begin to imagine a post-carbon world of climate justice, can we begin to create it now, while we strenuously resist the radical injustices involved in our rapid destruction of our common home? If not,

what cultural narratives, profoundly rooted in our ghostly unconsciousness, prevent us?

Notes

1. Hansen (Shabecoff, 1988), working for NASA and testifying before Congress,
   identified the greenhouse effect in 1988. Soon after, Roman Catholic feminist
   theologian Rosemary Radford Ruether published *Gaia and God: An Ecofeminist
   Theology of Earth Healing* (1992), anticipating by a quarter century much of
   what I am saying here, and of what the new encyclical proclaims. This *tour de
   force* provides a needed supplement, even corrective, perhaps, to my views.
2. Critiques of Cartesianism in psychoanalytic work, including meaning-oriented
   psychotherapies, include the work of Philip Cushman (1995, 2011), Robert
   Stolorow and George Atwood (1992), and many others. They recommend
   instead approaches such as contextualism, hermeneutics, phenomenology,
   complexity, and dynamic systems theories.
3. As Davis (2006) notes, such rationality belonged in the Greek view only to free
   men, not to slaves who made the leisure needed for theorizing possible. We
   might further note that the carbon-intensive industrial societies of the West
   were originally linked to African slavery.
4. The new encyclical criticizes this monism under another rubric: "When
   human beings place themselves at the centre, they give absolute priority to
   immediate convenience and all else becomes relative. Hence we should not be
   surprised to find, in conjunction with the omnipresent technocratic paradigm
   and the cult of unlimited human power, the rise of a relativism which sees
   everything as irrelevant unless it serves one's own immediate interests" (*Laudato Si*, #122). Psychoanalysts call this attitude infantile; it wants what it wants
   and wants it now.
5. Some would argue that knowing always totalizes and dominates, that when it
   seems peaceful, we actually find meeting (Buber & Kaufmann, 1970), responding (Levinas, 1969), non-reductionistic inquiry based on pluralistic and per-
   spectival assumptions.
6. Philosopher Judith Butler (Butler & Athanasiou, 2013) clearly links individualism, property, domination, and what she calls "precarity." She believes
   inequality and injustice to be inevitable in systems built primarily on individual rights to property. Many people and groups will be seen as leading
   dispensable and "ungrievable" lives.
7. Psychologist Janice Gump writes of slavery as transgenerationally transmitted
   trauma (Gump, 2010).
8. Naomi Klein (Klein, 2014) develops at length the story of the leadership indigenous peoples (First Nations) in Canada, the United States, and in Latin America are taking in resistance to the expansion of the most destructive forms of
   the fossil fuel industry: tar sands oil, fracking, and open pit mining. She cau-
   tions, however, that we who have colonized them and stolen their lands still
   owe them enormous debts.
9. Also reported in my recent *Nourishing the Inner Life of Clinicians and Humanitarians: The Ethical Turn in Psychoanalysis* (Orange, 2016).

10. Kohut's masterful book, *A German Generation: An Experiential History of the Twentieth Century* (T. A. Kohut, 2012), further makes it clear that the sense of belonging to elites, even if only semi-conscious, can make it impossible to see suffering others as fellow humans. We of the so-called first world who have largely created the climate crisis might take note.
11. Philip Cushman (2007), explaining Erich Fromm (1955, 1966), contributes another source of emotional freezing, namely, idolatry. "Worship takes on the quality of complete submission to idolatrous processes, an inability to question the dynamic or resist its power. Whether in the positive or the negative varieties, this dynamic of disavowal and worship is alienating and highly destructive. . . . Fromm used this concept to explain such noxious late modern-era social phenomena as consumerism, racism, and blind patriotism" (p. 77). Idolizing movie stars or demonizing African American males, both are deadening.
12. *Tikkun*, both a journal and a website, means fixing or rectification, and devotes itself, in the Jewish tradition, to repairing our broken world.
13. The 2010 U.S. Supreme Court decision made unlimited "big money" from corporations and unions available for political campaigns.
14. I recently learned that a single one-way flight from my home in California to New York uses all the carbon to which I am entitled for one year as a member of a climate just world. Every bit more that I use—for driving, flying, living—adds to global warming and comes on the backs of the world's poorest.
15. Its plenaries (Bill McKibben, Vandana Shiva, Wes Jackson, Sheri Liao, John Cobb, Herman Daly), section plenaries, program, and other follow-up, can be found on the Pando Populus website, which owes its name to the image of the 100 acres of quaking aspens in southern Utah, all growing from a single root, the world's largest organism (www.pandopopulus.com).
16. See my comments at (Orange, 2008).

References

Adams, W. (2015). Healing Our Dissociation from Body and Nature: Gestalt, Levinas, and Earth's Ethical Call. *British Gestalt Journal, 24*, 32–38.
Arendt, H. (1951). *The origins of totalitarianism* (1st ed.). New York: Harcourt.
Boswell, J., & Chapman, R. W. (2008). *Life of Johnson*. Oxford; New York: Oxford University Press.
Buber, M., & Kaufmann, W. A. (1970). *I and Thou*. New York: Scribner.
Butler, J. (2004). *Precarious life: The powers of mourning and violence*. London; New York: Verso.
Butler, J., & Athanasiou, A. (2013). *Dispossession: The performative in the political*. Malden, MA: Polity.
Catholic Church. Pope (2013– : Francis) (2015). *Encyclical on climate change and inequality: On care for our common home*. Brooklyn, NY: Melville House Publishing.
Coates, T.-N. (2015). *Between the world and me*. New York: Spiegel and Grau.
Cushman, P. (1995). *Constructing the self, constructing America: A cultural history of psychotherapy*. Boston: Addison-Wesley.
Cushman, P. (2007). A Burning World, an Absent God: Midrash, Hermeneutics, and Relational Psychoanalysis. *Contemp. Psychoanal, 43*, 47–88.

Cushman, P. (2011). So Who's Asking? Politics, Hermeneutics, and Individuality. In R. Frie & W. Coburn (Eds.), *Persons in context: The challenge of individuality in theory and practice* (pp. 21–40). London; New York: Routledge.

Davis, D. B. (2006). *Inhuman bondage: The rise and fall of slavery in the New World.* New York: Oxford University Press.

Figal, G. N. (2010). *Objectivity: The hermeneutical and philosophy.* Albany: State University of New York Press.

Figueroa, R. (2011). Indigenous Peoples and Cultural Losses. In J. Dryzek, R. Norgaard, & D. Schlosberg (Eds.), *The Oxford handbook of climate change and society* (pp. 232–247). Oxford, UK: Oxford University Press.

Fromm, E. (1955). *The sane society.* New York: Rinehart.

Fromm, E. (1966). *You shall be as gods; a radical interpretation of the Old Testament and its tradition.* New York: Holt.

Gadamer, H.-G., & Palmer, R. E. (2007). *The Gadamer reader: A bouquet of the later writings.* Evanston, IL: Northwestern University Press.

Gadamer, H.-G., Weinsheimer, J., & Marshall, D. G. (2004). *Truth and method* (2nd, rev. ed.). London; New York: Continuum.

Gardiner, S. M. (2010). *Climate ethics: Essential readings.* Oxford; New York: Oxford University Press.

Gardiner, S. (2011). Climate Justice. In J. Dryzek, R. Norgaard, & D. Schlosberg (Eds.), *The Oxford handbook of climate change and society* (pp. 309–322). Oxford, UK: Oxford University Press.

Gobodo-Madikizela, P. (2016). *Breaking intergenerational cycles of repetition: A global dialogue on historical trauma and memory.* Leverkusen, Deutschland: Budrich.

Gore, A., & Melcher Media (2006). *An inconvenient truth: The planetary emergency of global warming and what we can do about it.* Emmaus, PA: Rodale Press.

Gump, J. (2010). Reality Matters: The Shadow of Trauma on African American Subjectivity. *Psychoanalytic Psychology, 27*, 42–54.

Hansen, J. (2005). A Slippery Slope: How Much Global Warming Constitutes "Dangerous Anthropogenic Interference"? An Editorial Essay. *Climatic Change, 68*, 269–279.

Hansen, J. E. (2009). *Storms of my grandchildren: The truth about the coming climate catastrophe and our last chance to save humanity* (1st U.S. ed.). New York: Bloomsbury USA.

Hansen, J., Sato, M., Hearty, P., Ruedy, R., Kelley, M., Masson-Delmotte, V., . . . Lo, K.-W. (2015). Ice Melt, Sea Level Rise and Superstorms: Evidence from Paleoclimate Data, Climate Modeling, and Modern Observations That 2 °C Global Warming Is Highly Dangerous. *Atmospheric Chemistry and Physics, 15*, 20059–200179.

Hegel, G. W. F., Geraets, T. O. F., Suchting, W. A., & Harris, H. S. (1991). *The encyclopaedia logic, with the Zusätze: Part I of the encyclopaedia of philosophical sciences with the Zusätze.* Indianapolis: Hackett Pub. Co.

Hobbes, T., Gaskin, J. C. A., & NetLibrary Inc. (1998). *Leviathan Oxford World's Classics* (pp. lv, 508). Retrieved from http://www.columbia.edu/cgi-bin/cul/resolve?clio4245327

IEA, I. E. A. (2015). *World Energy Outlook Special Report 2015: Energy and Climate Change*. Retrieved from https://www.iea.org/publications/freepublications/publication/weo-2015-special-report-energy-climate-change.html

IPCC, I. P. o. C. C. (2014a). *Intergovernmental Panel on Climate Change (IPCC), Climate Change Synthesis Report for Policymakers*. Retrieved from https://www.ipcc.ch/pdf/assessment-report/ar5/syr/AR5_SYR_FINAL_SPM.pdf

IPCC, I. P. o. C. C. (2014b). *Climate Change 2014 Synthesis Report Summary for Policy Makers*. Retrieved from https://www.ipcc.ch/pdf/assessment-report/ar5/syr/AR5_SYR_FINAL_SPM.pdf

IPCC, I. P. o. C. C. (2014c). *Headline Statements 2014*. Retrieved from https://www.ipcc.ch/news_and_events/docs/ar5/ar5_syr_headlines_en.pdf

Jackson, W. (2010). *Consulting the genius of the place: An ecological approach to a new agriculture*. Berkeley: Counterpoint Press.

James, W. (1902). *The varieties of religious experience: A study in human nature*. New York: Longmans, Green, and Co.

James, W. (1977). *A pluralistic universe*. Cambridge, MA: Harvard University Press.

Jamieson, D. (2003). *A Companion to Environmental Philosophy Blackwell Companions to Philosophy Ser*. Retrieved from http://www.columbia.edu/cgi-bin/cul/resolve?clio10624092

Jamieson, D. (2014). *Reason in a dark time: Why the struggle against climate change failed—and what it means for our future*. Oxford, UK: Oxford University Press.

King, Martin Luther, Jr. (1986). I Have a Dream. In J. Washington (Ed.), *A testament of hope: The essential writings of Martin Luther King, Jr.* (pp. 217–220). San Francisco, CA: Harper Collins.

King, M. L., & Washington, J. M. (1986). A testament of hope: the essential writings of Martin Luther King, Jr. San Francisco: Harper & Row., p. 243. Dr. King used these words in at least two famous speeches.

Klein, N. (2014). *This changes everything: Capitalism vs. the climate* (1st Simon & Schuster hardcover ed.). New York: Simon & Schuster.

Knapton, S. (2015, June 19). Earth Has Entered Sixth Mass Extinction, Warn Scientists. *The Telegraph*. Retrieved from http://www.telegraph.co.uk/news/uknews/11687091/Earth-has-entered-sixth-mass-extinction-warn-scientists.html

Kohut, T. (2003). Psychoanalysis as Psychohistory or Why Psychotherapists Cannot Afford to Ignore Culture. *Annual Psychoanalysis, 31*, 225–236.

Kohut, T. A. (2012). *A German generation: An experiential history of the twentieth century*. New Haven, CT: Yale University Press.

Lasch, C. (1978). *The culture of narcissism: American life in an age of diminishing expectations*. New York: Norton.

Lear, J. (2006). *Radical hope: Ethics in the face of cultural devastation*. Cambridge, MA: Harvard University Press.

Lertzman, R. (2015). *Environmental melancholia: Psychoanalytic dimensions of engagement*. New York: Routledge.

Levinas, E. (1969). *Totality and infinity: An essay on exteriority*. Pittsburgh: Duquesne University Press.

Levinas, E. (1979). *Totality and infinity: An essay on exteriority.* Hague; Boston Hingham, MA: M. Nijhoff Publishers; Distributors for the U.S. and Canada, Kluwer Boston.

Levinas, E. (1981). *Otherwise than being: Or, beyond essence.* Hague; Boston Hingham, MA: M. Nijhoff Publishers; Distributors for the U.S. and Canada, Kluwer Boston.

Linderman, F. B., & Linderman, F. B. (1972). *Plenty-Coups, chief of the Crows.* New York: John Day Co.

Locke, J., Shapiro, I., & Locke, J. (2003). *Two treatises of government: And a letter concerning toleration.* New Haven, CT; London: Yale University Press.

Loewald, H. W. (1962). Internalization, Separation, Mourning, and the Superego. *Psychoanalytic Quarterly, 31,* 483–504.

Loewald, H. W. (1973). On Internalization. *International Journal of Psychoanalysis, 54,* 9–17.

Loewald, H. W. (1988). Termination Analyzable and Unanalyzable. *Psychoanalytic Study Child, 43,* 155–166.

Marshall, G. (2014). *Don't even think about it: Why our brains are wired to ignore climate change* (1st U.S. ed.). New York: Bloomsbury USA.

McKibben, B. (2010). *Eaarth: Making a life on a tough new planet* (1st ed.). New York: Time Books.

McKibben, B. (2014). *Oil and honey: The education of an unlikely activist* (1st St. Martin's Griffin ed.). New York: St. Martin's Griffin.

NASA (2008). *Where Should Humanity Aim?* Retrieved from http://www.giss.nasa.gov/research/briefs/hansen_13/

NOAA, N. O. a. A. A. (2015). *National Oceanic and Atmospheric Administration.* Retrieved from http://www.noaa.gov/

Ogden, T. (2010). On Three Forms of Thinking: Magical Thinking, Dream Thinking, and Transformative Thinking. *Psychoanalytic Quarterly, 79,* 317–347.

Orange, D. (2008). Radical Hope: Ethics in the Face of Cultural Devastation. *Psychoanlytic Psychology, 25,* 368–374.

Orange, D. (2016). *Nourishing the inner life of clinicians and humanitarians: The ethical turn in psychoanalysis.* London: Routledge.

Pascal, B., & Levi, H. (2008). *Pensées and other writings.* Oxford; New York: Oxford University Press.

Peperzak, A. T., & Levinas, E. (1993). *To the other: An introduction to the philosophy of Emmanuel Levinas.* West Lafayette, IN: Purdue University Press.

Plato, Cooper, J. M., & Hutchinson, D. S. (1997). *Complete works.* Indianapolis, IN: Hackett Pub. Co.

Rawls, J. (1971). *A theory of justice.* Cambridge, MA: Belknap Press of Harvard University Press.

Robinson, M. (2015, July 3). *Pathways That Respect Our Common Home.* Paper presented at the People and Planet First: The Imperative to Change Course. Retrieved from http://www.mrfcj.org/media/pdf/2015/SpeechMaryRobinson-Pathwaysthatrespectourcommonhome-03072015.pdf

Ryde, J. (in press). *A world in turmoil: Understanding trauma among refugees who flee from war, persecution and an unsustainable life.*

Sassenfeld, A. (2016). El Espacio Ermeneutico: Comprensión y espacialidad en la psicoterapia analítica intersubjetiva. London, Karnac.

Shabecoff, P. (1988, June 24). Global Warming Has Begun, Expert Tells Senate. *The New York Times.*

Shiva, V. (2005). *Globalization's new wars: Seed, water & life forms.* New Delhi: Women Unlimited.

Shiva, V. (2008). *Soil not oil: Environmental justice in an age of climate crisis.* Cambridge, MA: South End Press.

Shiva, V. (2010). *Staying alive: Women, ecology and survival in India.* New Delhi: Women Unlimited.

Shue, H. (2014). *Climate justice: Vulnerability and protection* (1st ed.). Oxford: Oxford University Press.

Stolorow, R. D. (2007). *Trauma and human existence: Autobiographical, psychoanalytic, and philosophical reflections.* New York: Analytic Press.

Stolorow, R. (2013). *Death, Afterlife, and Doomsday Scenario.* Retrieved from https://www.psychologytoday.com/blog/feeling-relating-existing/201312/death-afterlife-and-doomsday-scenario

Stolorow, R. D., & Atwood, G. E. (1992). *Contexts of being: The intersubjective foundations of psychological life.* Hillsdale, NJ: Analytic Press.

Straker, G. (2004). Race for Cover: Castrated Whiteness, Perverse Consequences. *Psychoanalytic Dialogues, 14,* 405–422.

Straker, G. (2011). Shaping Subjectivities: Private Memories, Public Archives. *Psychoanalytic Dialogues, 21,* 643–657.

The Time Is Now: Buddhist Declaration on Climate Change. (2015, May). Retrieved from http://fore.yale.edu/files/Buddhist_Climate_Change_Statement_5-14-15.pdf

Westphal, M. (1998). Levinas and the "Logic" of Solidarity. *Graduate Faculty Philosophy Journal, 20*(2), 297–319.

Chapter 2

Historical unconsciousness and the invisible present

Settler colonialism and chattel slavery

Unconscious and silent about the U.S. history of settler colonialism, ignorant and mute about our crimes of chattel slavery and racial domination, neither governments nor citizens can seriously tackle climate injustice until we confront this 400-year history.[1] This is my thesis. It accuses the "me," ever guilty and responsible, as we will find in Chapter 4, but locates the problems in a shared historical and narrative unconsciousness, in a "we." The thesis depends on history, culture, and psychoanalytic views of unconsciousness. Ambiguities remain. Let us nevertheless begin, contritely begging the help of those who can see what we cannot.

Blind to the history of our own ease in walking down the street unafraid, we remain trapped in the myth of whiteness so perfectly expressed by Ta-Nehisi Coates (Coates, 2015), who writes to his son about "white" people:

> Their new name [white] has no meaning divorced from the machinery of criminal power. The new people were something else before they were white—Catholic, Corsican, Welsh, Mennonite, Jewish . . . it must be said that washing the disparate tribes white, the elevation of the belief in being white, was not achieved through wine-tastings and ice-cream socials, but rather through the pillaging of life, liberty, labor, and land; through the flaying of backs; the chaining of limbs; the strangling of dissidents; the destruction of families; the rape of mothers; the sale

of children; and various other acts meant, first and foremost, to deny you and me the right to secure and govern our own bodies.

(pp. 7–8)

What we cannot fathom from our comfortable perspective, he can see clearly.

Origin of the uncanny and the intractable in human life, originating in life before language and distinctions, full of trouble and full of creativity, unconsciousness fascinates psychoanalysts. Freud studied our personal archeology, locating there the drives, instincts, and impulses, the love and hate mostly unknown to us. He also, in his later years, placed the origins of the personal unconscious in an original mythical story of ancestors who rose up against the father. Since Freud, every new school has rethought unconsciousness, but no one abandons it. Both the destructive and the creative in human life seem to originate out of our direct line of sight, and also out of our control. To make the unconscious conscious, or at least preconscious, according to the traditional view of psychoanalytic work, meant to bring this dark realm into the daylight and under the ego's control.

Most interesting rethinking, to my mind, comes from relational and intersubjective rethinking in contemporary psychoanalysis, with strong influences from developmental studies. Access to this "unthought known" (Bollas, 1987) comes from conversation, specifically the therapeutic dialogue and the parent–infant interaction studies. Intersubjective systems theory has given us the "prereflective unconscious," home of the organizing principles (Atwood & Stolorow, 2014; Stolorow & Atwood, 1992; Stolorow, Atwood & Brandchaft, 1987) or emotional convictions (Orange, 1995) patterning our lives, and derived from interactions with early caregivers. Relational psychoanalysis has shown us the "relational unconscious" (Bromberg, 2009) that belongs to both persons but to neither alone. "It is by allowing the boundary between self and other to become increasingly permeable that the patient-analyst relationship becomes in itself a therapeutic environment in which old truths can be reorganized into new patterns of self/other meaning" (p. 352), or as either Bion (Bion, 1959) or Loewald (Loewald, 1972) would have suggested by relinking what has been disconnected or never connected. This chapter works to link past and current injustices so that we may begin to feel their traumatic violence, as well as their ethical demand. Blindness to our ancestors' crimes, and to the ways we "whites" continue to live from these crimes, keeps the suffering of those already exposed to the devastation of climate crisis impossible for us to see or feel.

In another evocative formulation, Hans Loewald provided my favorite definition of unconsciousness, with implications, I believe, for climate justice. Explaining how psychoanalysis, the talking cure, does its therapeutic work, he wrote:

> The transference neurosis, in the technical sense of the establishment and resolution of it in the analytic process, is due to the blood of recognition which the patient's unconscious is given to taste—so that the old ghosts may reawaken to life. Those who know ghosts tell us that they long to be released from their ghost-life and led to rest as ancestors. As ancestors they live forth in the present generation, while as ghosts they are compelled to haunt the present generation with their shadow-life. Transference is pathological in so far as *the unconscious is a crowd of ghosts*, and this is the beginning of the transference neurosis in analysis: ghosts of the unconscious, imprisoned by defenses but haunting the patient in the dark of his defenses and symptoms, are allowed to taste blood, are let loose. In the daylight of analysis the ghosts of the unconscious are laid and led to rest as ancestors whose power is taken over and transformed into the newer intensity of present life, of the secondary process and contemporary objects.
>
> (Loewald, 1960, p. 29, emphasis added)

For the working psychoanalyst, these words evoke the uncanny experiences we know well: that more people inhabit the room than just the two of us, that each participant in the analytic process brings in ghosts who may still be causing trouble, neither named nor engaged, not yet laid to rest as ancestors. When the patient's "crowd of ghosts" evoke those of the analyst, or vice versa, impasses and enactments may ensue, leading in the best instances to resting ancestors, but often simply adding to the psychoanalytic literature, hoping to enlighten the community as to the location and activities of these unconscious ghosts.

For our purposes, let us imagine another crowd of ghosts inhabiting our ethical unconsciousness. Though single ones may live as well to cause trouble—Chapter 1 evoked Descartes and Locke—now let consider the historical unburied crimes, our collective ghosts, though largely unconscious, of settler colonialism and chattel slavery in the Americas, and especially in the United States, founded on the explicit ideal of human equality. I choose these, colonialism and slavery, because our habits of keeping these crimes—genocides before the term came to usage after World War II—hidden from ourselves may also be keeping us unaware of the impacts of climate change on people who live out of our daily sight. This chapter intends to make this connection clearer, and thus usable.

Settler colonialism

Well-meaning, hospitality-intending, we in the United States characterize ourselves as "a nation of immigrants," evoking impoverished Italians from Sicily and Calabria or Irish from the potato famine, as well as those fleeing religious and political persecution. But this expression hides as much as it tells. The explorers who first settled the Americas[2] came west, with the explicit blessing of the popes of the time, to claim all the gold, silver, and land, according to the doctrine of *Terra Nullius*, empty land, as if no one lived there. And soon the Spaniards, and the Portuguese, saw to it that no one did, except a few whom they baptized. Eduardo Galeano (Galeano, 1973), the master Uruguayan writer, details this history in *Open Veins of Latin America*, showing how Renaissance Europeans, followed by capitalists from the United States, have continually destroyed his land and people, eliminating their capacity for economic and political self-determination, reducing them to subsistence. "Murder by poverty," he calls it, detailing an inequality in 1970s Latin America much worse than the situation many of us abhor in the United States today. He writes:

Along the way we have even lost the right to call ourselves Americans, although the Haitians and Cubans appeared in history as a new people a century before the *Mayflower* pilgrims settled along the Plymouth coast. For the world today, America is just the United States; the region we inhabit is a sub-America, a second-class America of nebulous identity.

(p. 2)

The history in North America, from where I write, runs similarly, with two nations, England and France, competing to rule, replaced by the young United States with its "Manifest Destiny" and by an expansive Canada, destroying the indigenous peoples. Canada, it seems, has recently attempted much greater acknowledgment of its "First Nations" than we have done in the United States, where we name them "Native Americans," oblivious to the preference of most for being called by their tribal names, or simply "Indians."[3] Settler colonialism does not simply manage colonies as Britain did in India, arrogant as this process may be, but replaces the peoples living there, as in Australia and New Zealand, Canada, and what became the United States, as if the beings living there were not fellow human beings whose lives mattered at all. Judith Butler (Butler, 2010) would say these lives had been treated as "ungrievable." Calling ourselves "a nation of immigrants," we do not even notice their loss.

Consider the Hopi people, each year squeezed into a smaller and smaller area of northern Arizona, partly by the Navajos and partly by the whites (Spicer, 1962). Determined to survive and to protect their traditional and treasured cultural practices, language, and arts, they resisted Spanish colonization and conversion to Christianity, though peacefully (except for one final revolt). Unlike many other groups, they have been thought exotic, non-threatening, and their art valuable.

The Hopis, like many other tribal groups, however, could not match the might of the next set of conquerors from the United States, who, always knowing better, took their children away to the Indian schools by force. In the late 19th century, the school at Keams Canyon, only 35 miles from home for most, might as well have been a thousand miles away. Forcibly separated from their families, the children had to speak English, wear non-indigenous clothes, and were punished, sometimes by humiliating hair-cutting, for speaking their own languages or reverting to their traditional ways (James, 1974). To this day, the descendants of these children remember this period bitterly and with continuing distrust in whites and suspicion that we still place their cultural values and language at risk. Asked what the petroglyphs found inscribed on rocks throughout northern Arizona and New Mexico mean, guides say that no one knows. Hopis say: we know but we are not telling you. Our ancestors wrote those things.

Or consider Mexico City, the home of the astonishing Mexhicah (we call them Aztec) people who founded their city at Tenochtitlan. Like most tourists, I wanted to see the "most important places" when I recently visited. So my hosts took me to the enormous Spanish-era cathedral, built on top of an Aztec temple, right next to the Templo Major, the center of Aztec civilization, now being excavated by a team of archeologists. My host, whose mother belonged to one of the barely surviving indigenous groups, commented that the Spaniards didn't just want to take our land; they wanted to destroy us spiritually.

A few weeks later, my travels landed me in Madrid, where memories of Mexico led me to the *Museo de América*. Its exhibits tell, almost exclusively in Spanish, the story of colonization, with a collection of indigenous artifacts collected by the early conquerors. Though my impoverished Spanish may have hindered me, I found little account of the devastation caused by these marvelous exploits. The museum seems to waver between awareness and the desire to tell an exciting and glorious story of conquest to the children of Madrid, most of the visitors I saw there. A current exhibit, *Pacífico: España y la Aventura de la Mar del Sur* (Spain and the Adventure of the South Sea), shows the routes and story of the sea voyages. Part of the exhibit's description runs:

> The South Sea adventure is the history of the ocean routes, of the transformation of the Pacific into a means of communication. It is the history of invisible wakes that would become the return trails for people, trade, culture, and ideas, but also for drama and lack of understanding between strange worlds.
>
> (museum brochure, its translation)

In the palaces and churches I found, also with no acknowledgment of the human cost, the gold and silver and other wealth the conquerors brought back to Europe.[4]

Like the story of the Indian[5] schools, this history reflects systematic ethical unconsciousness, past and present. Living in its midst, living on land stolen from these people and robbed of their spirit, how can we notice the lives being destroyed now by economic colonialism, by our very own consumerism? Without interrogating my own historical and narrative unconsciousness (Freeman, 2014), I try to respond ethically to injustice toward the world's poorest, those dying of thirst and hunger, without any more capacity to see them than I have to see the back of my own head. My perspective, my ethical optic, is systematically distorted and occluded by my actual historical and cultural position. I did not choose to be born white, with all the advantages and automatic unconsciousness inherited from colonialism. My early schooling, together with popular movies and early television, taught me to regard colonists as holy and as strivers, with covered-wagon pioneers as heroes. Cowboys, cultural ideals, fought Indians, embodiment of evil. When we played "cowboys and Indians," only the disliked children took the Indian roles. Generally there were no roles at all for women, of course; we tomboy girls often had to play the disparaged Indians, to be killed in the end. None of us, even growing up in Oregon, knew any indigenous people personally; they had long since been moved to reservations, where they could no longer cause trouble for us children of superior people. Looking at these attitudes now, I am horrified, but realize that these human beings, full of rich culture and art, knowing how to live reverently on the earth, are still disappeared, both on the national stage and in our consciousness.

Now I write these words on a computer probably made in China, by people whose air is becoming completely unbreathable. I furiously lament the policies that privilege carbon-spewing cars over public transport and bicycles, here and in China, but who am I to blame others for wanting the advantages I take for granted? One street away from me, I walk or drive on Indian Hill Boulevard. Why Indian Hill? Because before my charming middle-class college town grew up, indigenous people, Tongva Indians lived here less than a mile from where I live. When the Spanish arrived to conquer what is now California, these indigenous people, first driven out, then gradually disappeared. More ethical unconsciousness as I use Indian Hill Boulevard every day. How can I become shocked by my own complacency?

Again, the ethical and ironic voice of Galeano, quoted by Isabel Allende in the preface to *Open Veins*: "We live in a world that treats the dead better than the living. We, the living are askers of questions and givers of answers, and we have other grave defects unpardonable by a system that believes death, like money, improves people" (1973, p. xi). Now the living must ask questions; we must listen closely to the voices of those who still speak for the dead from violence, from a perspective we cannot have. Close reading and close listening become ethical work, linking the crimes of the past with climate injustice, wreaking the same havoc now as our ancestors did on indigenous peoples.

Chattel slavery

Chattel slavery names the system, including in particular the African slave trade of the 15th through the 19th centuries, of claiming to own, buy and sell, inherit, and force to work—usually by extreme violence—human beings. Other forms of slavery, including those practiced by the Nazis and in the Soviet gulags, as well as forms of child labor, sex slavery, unspeakably reprehensible as they are and cause of untold human suffering, are not under direct discussion here. My argument is that chattel slavery, the "peculiar institution" that formed the United States Constitution, giving outsized power to the slaveholding South, and haunting us to this day (Blackmon, 2009; Davis, 2006), has dulled our moral consciousness to the point of unconsciousness. What we do not know, really profoundly and extensively and personally know, Freud taught us, we are bound to repeat. Together with the colonialist past we all share, this history of slavery and its ongoing effects, of which we rarely speak, blinds us to the misery that our carbon-and-methane-spewing lifestyles are creating in the Global South. We are repeating. This is my thesis in this chapter.

David Brion Davis (Davis, 2006) explains that the New England and Virginian colonists could never have fought off and maintained their independence from England without the prosperity produced in the slaveholding South. Thus, when it came time to write a constitution, the Southerners exercised an outsized influence on the new government's structure. They wanted to be sure that the North's greater population could never take command through a true popular sovereignty, possibly challenging the system of slavery. We owe the Electoral College, according to Davis, to their influence, and they elected most of the early presidents. George Washington and Thomas Jefferson owned slaves, for example. The cruelty of the system, in separating families through sale, in prohibiting slaves from learning to read, in endless whippings and lashings, not to mention rapes, are detailed in Davis's volume and in his other work. For many of us, this history became real in the recent film, *Twelve Years a Slave*, making us realize that massive human rights violations have not occurred only in Germany, Austria, Chile, and South Africa, for example. We in the United States live every day from the history and continuance of precarity (Butler, 1990) generated by the conscious and unconscious racism with which Ta-Nehisi Coates confronts us. Writing to his son, he reminds us:

> enslavement is not a parable. It is damnation. It is the never-ending night. And the length of that night is most of our history. Never forget that we were enslaved in this country longer than we have been free. Never forget that for 250 years black people were born into chains—whole generations followed by more generations who knew nothing but chains.
>
> (p. 70)

Historically, the compensation question[6] arose, only with respect to the perpetrators, not the victims, of the slave system. Since few, even during and after the Civil War, saw the blacks as human brothers and sisters, no one thought to wonder if they deserved some payback for what they had unjustly suffered. Instead, within a few years, large numbers had been re-enslaved through an unjust penal system detailed by Douglas Blackmon (Blackmon, 2009) in *Slavery by Another Name*. The rest suffered under Jim Crow, an utterly dehumanizing set of human rights violations also called segregation. With official segregation outlawed, economic and social segregation keep us separated to this day, with the great-grandchildren of slaves in continued abjection. As Bryan Stevenson, tireless fighter for the unjustly incarcerated (Stevenson, 2014), writes in his foreword to Jim Wallis's *America's Original Sin: Racism, White Privilege, and the Bridge to a New America* (Wallis, 2016), "Involuntary servitude was banned by the Thirteenth Amendment to the U.S. Constitution, but nothing was done to confront the ideology of white supremacy" (p. xii). Indeed, shamefully, despite their origins in common with New England abolitionism and early support from Frederick Douglass, the white suffragists refused to make common cause with their black suffragist sisters in seeking the vote for women after the Civil War.

Important for our argument, whites, or as Ta-Nehisi Coates (Coates, 2015) aptly characterizes us, "Americans who believe that they are white" (p. 6), generally show incomprehension for, or indifference to, the ongoing struggles of their sisters and brothers of color, the struggling migrants who want to live among us, and the indigenous peoples we have rendered invisible. We seem incapable of imagining that we bear any historical responsibility for their plight, that we continue to benefit from it by living in a way that requires and creates an underclass, or that we might be obligated to do anything about it. Blinded by and to the presumptions created by our "whiteness," how could we possibly see the impact of climate crisis on our neighbors?

These questions, of course, open a large space of discourse on whiteness, an area my colleague Lynne Jacobs (Jacobs, 2014a, 2014b) studies in relation to psychotherapy. Of course, in a Wittgensteinian "family resemblance," the meanings of 'white' and 'whiteness' vary with the discourses in which they are used. Demographically, white usually means Caucasian, excluding Africans, Asians, especially South Asians, and people of mixed blood everywhere. But even this usage hides a terrible history: according to the notorious "one-drop" rule, anyone with the smallest possible amount of black heritage should be subject to the direst discrimination, just as under Hitler, a drop of Jewish blood meant deportation and death. (Propaganda posters from Nazi Germany depict Jews as black.) What of today, when our cities are full of people speaking dozens of languages and people of every possible color? Are impoverished Caucasians "white"? Many more questions remain. For the purposes of my argument here, however, I join Coates in viewing whiteness as the state of mind of "people who believe they are white," no matter what their skin color. This state of mind, more or less conscious, includes a sense of entitlement to walk down the street unmolested, to drive without being stopped arbitrarily and to be treated decently if stopped, to walk into a shop without being scrutinized, to live without fear that comes from knowing others see me as dark-skinned. All these entitlements should belong to everyone, of course; whiteness means taking them for granted without realizing I could not feel them without the underlying sense of being white. Coates asks where this "white" sense came from, and what maintains it. His challenging answer? Violence. My question asks whether living in a culture that tolerates, even encourages, violence toward people we consider non-white, we can possibly feel the racism inherent in climate injustice, in the effects of a carbon-profligate life on the world's poorest people.

Psychoanalysis again: the capacity for concern

Winnicott (1965) believed the capacity for concern for others evolved in a good-enough developmental situation. Concern, he wrote, "refers to the fact that the individual *cares,* or *minds,* and both feels and accepts responsibility" (p. 73). He explained that much had already happened before the stage of concern. The baby has gradually separated itself out from fusion with the environmental mother, though she remained important. Now the mother has become an other, what psychoanalysts call an object. Along the way, according to Winnicott, she could be treated ruthlessly, like a toy to be thrown on the floor. Now this mother is an other like the baby, with feelings and a life of her own. Still crucial as the environment-mother, providing safety, nourishment, and care, she now requires respect and concern. Ruthless treatment of this mother brings guilt. In a favorable developmental situation, with an ordinary capable mother,

> The infant is now becoming able to be concerned, to take responsibility for his own instinctual impulses and the functions that belong to them. This provides one of the fundamental constructive elements of play and work. But in the developmental process, it was the opportunity to contribute [care] that enabled concern to be within the child's capacity.
>
> (p. 77)

These developmental considerations enable us psychoanalysts to wonder where our capacity for concern begins and ends. Winnicott gave us at least one theory for its beginning, but did not mark its extent. Is the field of our vision opened and occluded in systematic ways by personal and collective history? This chapter has begun to suggest, that, beyond the forms of unconsciousness that every psychoanalyst studies every day, each of us suffers from specific limitations on our capacity for concern shaped not only by the limitations of the parents to whom we were born, but by those of the culture—including schools, religious groups, media, politics—that have formed us (Cushman, 2011). Outside our awareness, we have learned to take for granted that systematic injustices are simply the way things are, not that they have been deliberately created and organized, that we participate in prolonging them, constantly benefitting from them.

So perhaps we need a new Winnicott now, to write of extending our capacity for concern before so many more millions, in the climate crisis described in Chapter 1, die from our indifference, fear, and hatred. Social psychologists have conducted endless experiments to confirm what we suspect: that cruelty and indifference become easier at a distance or in the face of great numbers. They have also demonstrated that people feel better when they emerge from indifference and engage in helping others. But this research tells us only what we already know; it does not move us toward the engagement we need with climate crisis and global poverty. Even our psychoanalytic conferences and webinars are largely inward-looking, still discussing sex while our world dies from hunger, racism, guns, bombs, and rapidly rising sea levels.

Expanding concern and empathy

Having entered psychoanalysis through self psychology, I retain, in spite of my philosophical bones, a certain affection for the concept and practice of empathy. The English word *empathy* translates the German *Einfühlung*, "feeling into." One feels into nature, into a work of art, into the feelings of others. Unfortunately, however, with all its benevolent intentions, the word has carried, both in German and in English, connotations that a clear-thinking, pragmatic, relational, much less an intersubjective systems phenomenologist devoted to understanding personally organized worlds of experience, would hesitate to accept. It may, or may not, depending on definitions, imply an individual mysteriously reading the mind of another individual. As a finely tuned capacity, it may, as Heinz Kohut warned us, be put to good or evil purposes. It may imply feeling all and doing nothing, hardly an ethical approach in psychoanalysis or to life in general. So we need either (1) to define empathy so carefully that few could possibly misunderstand or misuse it, (2) to scrap it in favor of other leading ideas, or (3) to integrate its values into what we may now hold. To tip my hand, I incline toward the third alternative.

Heinz Kohut clearly favored the first alternative, defining empathy as our only entry point into the psychological life of those we seek to serve. He claimed, indeed, that empathy was a way of knowing—I might say imagining—that defined the psychological method of cure we call psychoanalysis.

I will suggest two paths for a psychoanalysis interested in surmounting some of the difficulties in ordinary empathy discourse: (1) a philosophical hermeneutics of dialogue or conversation, and (2) an ethics of pre-primordial responsibility for the other whom we serve. Separately and together, these complexify without abandoning the values inhering in the empathy talk many of us still cherish.

Most associated with the name of Hans-Georg Gadamer (1900–2002), philosophical hermeneutics refuses the classic idea of empathy for its subjectivism, that is, for its reliance on the idea that one mind enters the mind of the other. Instead, we learn to engage in conversation, unpredictable yet always truth-seeking, anticipating completion but never finished, playful yet utterly serious, always concerned with feeling but seeking to know the *Sache selbst*, the thing itself, the matter at hand. Hermeneutics sees conversation as our best approach to understanding. Unconsciousness, so dear to psychoanalytic sensibility, appears in philosophical hermeneutics as preconception and prejudice, what we take for granted until dialogue and conversation makes us more aware. (Readers of intersubjective systems theories will recognize here unconscious organizing principles, developmentally formed relational expectancies, or emotional convictions, as I like to call them.) Those of us concerned with the "ethical turn" in psychoanalysis will hear our inevitable prejudices as shaping our cultural biases, our presumptions of racial, sexual, class, and cultural privilege, as forms of unconsciousness seriously to worry us. Dialogic hermeneutics, not restricted to the dyad but often beginning there, takes the other's voice at least as seriously as our own, finding there a source of learning and self-correction. Listening well helps us to hold our theories lightly, as the pragmatists admonish us, and to test our empathic imagination in dialogue.

We can find in phenomenological ethics, the claim of a pre-primordial responsibility to the other, a second resource for improving traditional concepts of empathy. Once we have, in the face of another's suffering and of massive social injustices, not to mention the wanton destruction of our planet, heard Cain's question, "Am I my brother's keeper?" we are indicted. Feeling the other's plight, we can no longer stand by indifferent. We were born into responsibility. "I am guilty/responsible for all, and before all, and I more than all the others" we read repeatedly in *The Brothers Karamazov*. In the Hebrew scriptures we read that the widow, the orphan, and the stranger are our sisters and brothers. Later we hear "Blessed are the poor . . ." Chapter 4 will explore in more depth the possibilities of this radical ethics for confronting privilege and injustice so that we may respond to the extreme suffering already being generated by the climate crisis.

Now what, you may ask, has this "ethical" to do with psychoanalysis? I would claim that throughout its history, psychoanalysis has included people who placed the poor, the marginalized, and the devastated at the center of their work, and that its restriction to the middle and upper classes has been a deformation. We can think of Ferenczi, working with outcasts before he even met Freud, of Suttie reminding us of needs for tenderness, of Fairbairn working with the walking wounded returned from wars, of Winnicott with his delinquents, of Kohut including in theory and practice those long considered unanalyzable. Today there are more, known to many of us, studying white privilege, extreme inequality, immigration, effects of colonialism, class shame, climate crisis, and so on, with their devastating psychological and sociocultural effects.

The ethical turn, taken together with the profoundly intersubjective/relational attitudes described as dialogical, accords well with the values I have most treasured in the psychoanalytic self-psychological tradition, even as I have tried to expand its theory and practice toward a more explicit focus on history and culture. These include: (1) Despite what some consider an individualist emphasis in classical self psychology (Richardson & Fowers, 1999), despite perhaps its underemphasis on history and culture in clinical theory, I believe this approach, rejecting mechanistic and reductionistic notions, has helped to restore a humanitarian voice to psychoanalysis, loudly protesting the treatment of human beings as specimens and diagnoses; (2) Self psychology, in all its variations, has affirmed relatedness and interdependence as the basic human condition, seeing the sense of self as emergent from, and ever embedded in, the human world; (3) Self psychology has attempted to remain experience-near in its theorizing and practice; (4) Self psychology has legitimized care, compassion, even tenderness in psychotherapy and psychoanalysis; and (5) Self psychology, with its acute awareness of the many forms of shame and degradation, has placed the restoration of human dignity in the center of the therapeutic project. Even though I no longer describe myself as a self psychologist, or as belonging to any psychoanalytic denomination, but rather as a psychoanalyst/philosopher attempting to become a human being, the values I learned in my early years, exposed to those who had worked with Heinz Kohut, profoundly influenced me.

Sometimes our values are embodied best and taught to us again, by others outside psychoanalysis. Recently my 77-year-old brother-in-law needed a risky cancer surgery in a Southern city, hit by a record-breaking ice and snowstorm. This city does not have a single snowplow. His famous surgeon called early that morning to say his office would be closed and he could do the surgery first thing in the morning. We, however, were isolated on a hill several miles away and had no way to reach the hospital. No problem, said this surgeon, he was from the North, had a four-wheel drive, and would come to pick us up. He did, carried out the successful surgery, and also offered to drive my husband and me home whenever we were ready. When I thanked him, he said simply, "I couldn't let him worry any longer about this surgery."

If this be empathy, practical and unmysterious, unpretentious in the service of the other, I will have it.

The superiority complex

Playing on the old talk of inferiority complexes and low self-esteem, we might consider whether Europe and North America, especially we in the United States, suffer from a superiority complex. Symptoms of such a "complex" might include (1) the presumption that we own land stolen from indigenous peoples who lived upon it communally just because we bought it from people who "owned" it before us; (2) the presumption that the ways we who think ourselves as white do things are the right ways; (3) the presumption that others worldwide should learn English, while we have no obligation to learn Spanish or other widely spoken languages; (4) a general insensitivity to our own arrogance and sense of superiority, easily degenerating into violence against those we consider inferior; (5) an incapacity to imagine ourselves into the predicament of those to whom we feel superior, thus a blunting of empathy and compassion; (6) a sense that the earth belongs to us, the so-called whites, and that others, "they" exist to serve our economic interests: to mine the minerals we want or need, to make us cheap clothes, to work at below poverty wages, and so on. This complex, with its embedded assumptions, largely unconscious and invisible, forms a web of life, generating comfort among those who carry it and creating death and fury among those we dominate. We do not know that we suffer from it in our fundamental humanity.

Analyzing this unconscious sense of superiority with its careful cultivation in the German Bunds of the 1920s, historian Thomas Kohut suggests that learning from childhood that one belongs to a superior group easily prepared Germans for Nazi racist ideology.

They could not protect their Jewish, Roma, and Sinti neighbors because they had long learned to see them as not really German, and thus not fully human. As Kohut (Kohut, 2012), son of the famous psychoanalyst Heinz Kohut, explains, empathy-formed responsiveness to the other's endangerment and suffering becomes impossible from the position of superiority.[7] "They did not have the frail courage to look into our eyes," wrote Primo Levi (Levi, 1989, p. 169) of those who watched the boxcars roll by to extermination camps, and of those who saw the few return. Instead, since these miserable others never possessed human eyes for the superior ones, the acknowledgment had already become outside the possible.

Something similar occurs with the legacies of colonialism and slavery. The indigenous people and others of color whom we "whites," like the Germans, have reduced to sub-humans have no capacity to evoke our compassion. We cannot look into their eyes, and see people who suffer as we do, and who suffer from injustices we create. Invisible. Why do "they" hate us, we wonder. What do "they" want?

Similarly, as climate scientist Kevin Anderson explains in an interview at the Paris climate talks (https://www.youtube.com/watch?v=svlU6p0gHgo), those already being destroyed by our carbon-intensive lives in the Global North meet a similar indifference. "Let them eat cake," commented his interlocutor, Professor Hugh Hunt. Considering bioengineering far too risky, Hunt believes that only if the global rich immediately and radically cut back our consumption of everything—everything I do depends on carbon, he says—and governments immediately begin to redo infrastructure, do the Paris agreements have any hope of making a difference.

Without the scientific and technical expertise of Hunt and Anderson, but sharing Anderson's ethical and political concerns, I would guess, that here in North America at least, facing our racism, finding some "frail courage" to acknowledge our "original sin" of slavery and colonial destruction (Wallis, 2016) will be necessary if we are to take on climate injustice. *Climate injustice is racism*, unconscious perhaps, but racism all the same, inherited of course, but now our guilt and our responsibility. Just as Germans my age never belonged to the Nazi party or actually perpetrated the Shoah (they are called the *Nachgeborene*, born late), I have never owned slaves or personally displaced Algonquins or Crow or Hopis or others. Nevertheless, living from these crimes, I am guilty and responsible to the victims and their descendants, and must involve myself in a profound conversion.

How does one convert? Were I German, I would find out, as Roger Frie has done, everything possible about my own family's involvement in the Nazi machine, and about what happened to the regime's victims. I would read the literature extensively and intensively even if it gave me nightmares, while attempting to meet and listen to the victims. Instead, my task, I have come to believe, is to learn everything I can about slavery, racism, and their effects on my darker-skinned neighbors, from books, from these neighbors themselves. I need to know the violent details of colonial domination and of slavery, working to imagine myself in the lives of the victims. I need to feel the despair of those released from literal slavery, only to face hatred, unjust incarceration, police violence, lack of access to basics that, even growing up poor, I took for granted. "Black lives matter" means they have not mattered enough, if at all, to me and other "whites" who mindlessly assume we matter more. Conversion means a U-turn, turning me toward the faces of those whose devastation implicates me in ways I have not been able to see or hold in mind. Without such conversion, we privileged ones will not be able to care enough about the human effects of climate change to decarbonize our lives in the radical ways needed even to reach the 2% goal that will leave billions miserable or dead. We simply will not place our comforts at risk.

In our last chapter, we will listen for an even more radical call, hoping to break through our moral fog. Meanwhile we must recall from Chapter 1 that mourning remains the work to be done before ethical growth becomes possible. Perhaps keeping our indigenous people invisible and our people of color abject has short-circuited mourning, not so much theirs as ours. Blues and gospel music remind us that we, not the victims, are the ones who forget the trauma of slavery, like all trauma lived through generations. We have Holocaust memorials, memorials that stun, but none (to my knowledge) to slavery or to the elimination of peoples native to the very places in which we now live. Only recently did New Yorkers realize that a slave graveyard lay beneath lower Manhattan. Did we gather and mourn, as if we knew that horrors had befallen our own people? I do not remember that we did. We celebrate Columbus Day and Thanksgiving, the festivals of our colonial past, rarely mourning for those we displaced, to minimize more than a little.

Loewald, to repeat, calling up the ghosts of the unconscious, taught us that mourning our losses is the condition for the possibility of moral development, for the development of conscience (superego in the old language). The problem is, we must perceive these losses, due to slavery and colonialism, as *our* losses. As long as we continue to regard these losses as belonging to others less human than we are, we will not be able to recognize the depth and extent of those losses, our implication in them, or to mourn them individually or communally. We will not be able to develop the kind of conscience, or consciousness, that regards people of color everywhere as our brothers and sisters if we remain blocked in our process of mourning.

Mourning, further, means internalizing the values of the lost ones while we let them go. To do this we will need to know them better. Working to acquaint ourselves with the vast cultural contributions of people of color and indigenous peoples, with their music, art, and spirituality, for example, may help us to mourn and internalize. Richer ourselves, then, we may find ourselves both grateful and guilty/responsible toward those our ancestors and we ourselves have harmed. Mourning, seriously and extensively, including allowing ourselves to be taught, may expand our capacity for concern, in turn expanding our capacity to take on the challenges of climate justice.

Notes

1. At the end of World War II a similar task confronted Germans who could see only the rubble and their own suffering, not its causes brought on by their own crimes (cf. Frie [2016]).

2. My Latin American colleagues tell me that our habit in the United States of calling ourselves "Americans" erases them.

3. I am grateful to my neighbor Jack Jackson, a Seneca, for reminding me of this preference, one I had heard strongly voiced by Hopis too.

4. My Spanish friends and colleagues seem much more aware than this paragraph suggests.

5. Again I note that, differing from Canada's "First Peoples," most older indigenous people here want to be called their tribal names, or generally, "Indian." Younger ones often prefer "Native American." Only sensitivity in the situation resolves this. http://blog.nmai.si.edu/main/2011/01/introduction-1st-question-american-indian-or-native-american.html

6. Fortunately, Ta-Nehisi Coates foregrounds this urgent challenge to our somnolence once again (Coates, 2014).

7. Writing of the oversimplification involved in simply dividing perpetrators from "indifferent" bystanders, Kohut writes: "Whereas indifferent human beings do not carry out genocide, people lacking in empathy can persecute, deport, and exterminate or stand by, wordlessly, silently, passively, watching the persecution, deportation, and extermination. Neither perpetrators nor bystanders could imagine themselves in the place of the Jews. Jews were for both . . . 'another world'" (pp. 170–171).

References

Atwood, G. E., & Stolorow, R. D. (2014). *Structures of subjectivity: Explorations in psychoanalytic phenomenology and contextualism*. London; New York: Routledge, Taylor & Francis Group.

Bion, W. R. (1959). Attacks on Linking. *International Journal of Psychoanalysis, 40*, 308–315.

Blackmon, D. A. (2009). *Slavery by another name: The re-enslavement of Black Americans from the Civil War to World War II*. New York: Anchor Books.

Bollas, C. (1987). *The shadow of the object: Psychoanalysis of the unthought known*. New York: Columbia University Press.

Bromberg, P. (2009). Truth, Human Relatedness, and the Analytic Process: An Interpersonal/Relational Perspective. *International Journal of Psychoanalysis, 90*, 3347–3361.

Butler, J. (1990). *Gender trouble: Feminism and the subversion of identity*. New York: Routledge.

Butler, J. (2010). *Frames of war: When is life grievable?* London; New York: Verso.

Coates, T.-N. (2015). *Between the world and me*. New York: Spiegel and Grau.

Cushman, P. (2011). So Who's Asking? Politics, Hermeneutics, and Individuality. In R. Frie & W. Coburn (Eds.), *Persons in context: The challenge of individuality in theory and practice* (pp. 21–40). New York; London: Routledge.

Davis, D. B. (2006). *Inhuman bondage: The rise and fall of slavery in the New World*. New York: Oxford University Press.

Freeman, M. P. (2014). *The priority of the other: Thinking and living beyond the self*. Oxford, UK: Oxford University Press.

Frie, R. (2016). *Not in My Family: German Memory and the Holocaust.* London: Oxford University Press.

Galeano, E. (1973). *Open veins of Latin America: Five centuries of the pillage of a continent.* New York: Monthly Review Press.

Jacobs, L. (2014a). Circumstance of Birth: Life on the Color Line. *Psychoanalytic Inquiry, 34,* 746–758.

Jacobs, L. (2014b). Learning to Love White Shame and Guilt: Skills for Working as a White Therapist in a Racially Divided Country. *International Journal of Psychanalytic Self Psychology, 9,* 297–312.

James, H. C. (1974). *Pages from Hopi history.* Tucson: University of Arizona Press.

Kohut, T. A. (2012). *A German generation: An experiential history of the twentieth century.* New Haven, CT: Yale University Press.

Levi, P. (1989). *The drowned and the saved.* New York: Vintage International.

Loewald, H. W. (1960). On the Therapeutic Action of Psycho-Analysis. *International Journal of Psychoanalysis, 41,* 16–33.

Loewald, H. W. (1972). The Experience of Time. *The Psychoanalytic Study of the Child, 27,* 401–410.

Orange, D. M. (1995). *Emotional understanding: Studies in psychoanalytic epistemology.* New York: Guilford Press.

Richardson, F. C., & Fowers, B. (1999). *Re-envisioning psychology: Moral dimensions of theory and practice.* San Francisco, CA: Jossey-Bass.

Spicer, E. H. (1962). *Cycles of conquest: The impact of Spain, Mexico, and the United States on the Indians of the Southwest, 1533–1960.* Tucson: University of Arizona Press.

Stevenson, B. (2014). *Just mercy: A story of justice and redemption.* New York: Spiegel & Grau.

Stolorow, R. D., & Atwood, G. E. (1992). *Contexts of being: The intersubjective foundations of psychological life.* Hillsdale, NJ: Analytic Press.

Stolorow, R. D., Atwood, G., & Brandchaft, B. (1987). *Psychoanalytic treatment: An intersubjective approach.* Hillsdale, NJ: Analytic Press.

Wallis, J. (2016). *America's original sin: Racism, white privilege, and the bridge to a new America.* Grand Rapids: Brazos Press.

Winnicott, D. W. (1965). *The maturational processes and the facilitating environment: Studies in the theory of emotional development.* New York: International Universities Press.

Chapter 3

Beyond evasion
Psychoanalysis for the climate crisis

"It takes one to know one," chant children in response to insulting taunts. We psychoanalysts, experts at calling out the defenses and evasions of others, have notably excelled at avoidance in the face of crisis ourselves. Beginning with Freud, who long underestimated the Nazi threat, continuing through the British Society's "Controversial Discussions," to our own near silence in a "burning world" (Cushman, 2007), when it comes to our own peril, we have long been specialists in evasion.[1]

Let us admit it up front. Organized psychoanalysis holds a deplorable record in the face of moral emergencies. Our lack of civil courage has been stunning. In addition to the examples of Freud in the 1930s and of the self-absorbed British Society, we may consider the extensive collaboration of German psychoanalysts with the Nazi regime (Cocks, 1997) and the silence of organized psychoanalysis in the face of the U.S. resort to torture in the aftermath of the 9–11 attacks. Psychoanalyst Stephen Reisner, a true hero, has led the efforts to find out just how extensively involved were psychologists, with the blessing of the American Psychological Association (to which thousands of us psychoanalysts belong, and from which a few resigned in protest) in the Bush torture programs.[2] A very few other psychoanalysts have been seriously concerned since before 2008 (Boulanger, 2008; Grand, 2008; Soldz, 2008; Summers, 2008). We now know that leaders of the APA collaborated with the CIA and the Department of Defense to plan and justify torture of our fellow human beings for many years, while members actually helped to do it. The ethical corruption ran deeper, and more extensively, than almost anyone imagined. Most of us remained indifferent, or what is morally equivalent, silent.[3]

Once again, however, we face a crisis arguably equivalent in scale to that generated by Hitler. The National Socialists threatened, not only genocide—an intention becoming gradually fully evident—but also world domination. They menaced the very possibility of civilized, democratic, human dignity-oriented common life. Within two years they had already dominated eastern and western Europe. Next they formed an alliance with Japan to attack the United States, to disable any effective opposition. They wanted to possess Russia for its seemingly endless *Lebensraum*, a greater Germany.[4]

Although the genocides and other crimes against humanity did not rouse resistance or even much attention, the threat of Hitler ruling London and North America changed everything. We mobilized, converting everything to the war effort. In other words, we in the so-called civilized world have faced total existential threat before, and responded totally. Britons stopped driving cars. North Americans and Britons resorted to rationing, and transformed all their industries to meet the threat.[5] We know the drill, even though the psychoanalysts kept hiding and arguing in their cellars.

At this moment we face, as in the Nazi period, an imminent threat to our very existence as a minimally just civilization, except that now we have inflicted the crisis on ourselves and even more immediately, on the world's poorest, by our consumerist ways and by our addiction to the comforts provided by fossil fuels. It requires every resource available to wake us up and mobilize us to wake up our leaders as well. A few psychoanalysts have begun to speak. A clarion voice from the UK, Sally Weintrobe, has edited the first collection of papers on our topic, many by scientific experts but others by psychoanalysts (Weintrobe, 2012), mostly Kleinians and Bionians. These papers, reminding us in unequivocal tones of inherent human destructiveness, concentrate on many forms of denial and "splitting," explaining why people generally find it so difficult to perceive climate change even when they are already affected by it, or if they do, why they remain immobilized. We must hope to see soon a companion volume from relational psychoanalysis, including self psychology and the intersubjectivities. Joseph Dodds has contributed *Psychoanalysis and Ecology at the Edge of Chaos* (Dodds, 2011), using the resources of complexity theory and of neo-Kleinian psychoanalysis to warn us of attacks on linking (Bion, 1959), allowing us to keep climate change only semi-conscious, unlinked to any usable sense of responsibility, non-integrated. (I might say, with Christopher Bollas (1987), that it remains an unthought known.) As a capable reviewer (Marks-Tarlow, 2012) has pointed out, Dodds's book, while potentially discourse-changing, fails to include the voices of post-Freudian North American relationalists and contextualists including intersubjective systems theorists (D. M. Orange, Atwood, & Stolorow, 1997) and prophets like Philip Cushman (Cushman, 2007). Though this book does disappoint in some ways, it also brings the attention of psychoanalysts to this crisis and to their potential contribution to its understanding and solution. Just as my work goes to publication, comes social scientist Renee Lertzman's (2015) psychoanalytically voiced (mainly Kleinian) book on environmental melancholia. Against apathy as explanatory frame for general inaction, she uses melancholic loss of the developmental potential found in true mourning. Her theory fits well with the view I developed in Chapter 2, though it omits the links to mourning colonialism and slavery, so that we continue to live them out.

From the United States, an early and clear voice (Bodnar, 2008) comes from the consulting room, as Susan Bodnar hears the dying world echoed in the despair of her patients. Emphasizing the enveloping and pervasive role of environment in the psyche, and recommending a sensory reconnection to our environment, she believes the environmental movements need to take what she calls a "psychological turn" from cognitive to embodied knowing of our interconnectedness. U.S. analyst Elizabeth Allured reminds us that Harold Searles wrote of our embeddedness in the "nonhuman environment" long ago (H. F. Searles, 1960), and warned of our unconsciousness in the face of what he already saw as "environmental crisis" (H. Searles, 1972). Most of us, however, know Searles the proto-relationalist, and never caught this aspect of his thinking. I must admit that his *Nonhuman Environment* book has been sitting unread on my shelf for many years, and I had never until recently made the connection.

Another emerging and potentially important psychoanalytic resource comes from Judith Anderson's website for the Climate Psychology Alliance (CPA). I cannot recommend it too strongly as a way for clinicians to keep up on the latest science and to make contacts with concerned others.

Except for Weintrobe, and now in the CPA website, I still miss in the psychoanalytic discourses, and in those psychotherapeutic worlds with which I am familiar, an adequate sense of urgency.[6] Psychoanalysts can either keep on quietly working, eyes and ears wide shut, and remain part of the problem, or we can use all the resources of our profession to become part of the solution. This chapter will outline some of these conceptual resources, and propose some practical steps, mostly on the part of organized psychoanalysis, that could contribute to turning us around. Without discounting the suggestions of colleagues writing from other psychoanalytic traditions, and well aware that my perspective remains only a perspective, I focus on the contributions of shame, and of shame-based envy, to the production of intransigent and competitive consumerism. My practical suggestions are meant only to "prime the pump." Others more creative than I, and possibly more practical, instead of simply calling them unworkable, should propose better ideas of their own.

Double-mindedness to single-mindedness

Commonly we speak of ourselves as being "in denial" about various unpleasant realities: our unavoidable death, our health risks increased by our own behavior, and most recently, about the looming catastrophe of climate change. Psychoanalysis, in its various theoretical traditions, teaches us more nuanced views. Paul Hoggett (in Weintrobe, 2012) applies his conception of the perverse social defense, borrowed from John Steiner's (Steiner, 1993) account of perversion as not coming to terms with impending loss, to describe the way we hide from what we do not want to know. Stanley Cohen (in Weintrobe, 2012) differentiates forms of denial: literal, interpretative, and implicatory. All three forms operate to prevent genuine engagement with the climate crisis, though interpretation of what we know, with its implications for what we must do, if we are not to suffer unthinkably dire consequences, remains hardest to bear in mind. Others tell us that living in virtual universes where everything becomes a handheld video game prevents us from allowing ourselves to know that some things—rising temperatures, for example—are real and have consequences. Our narcissistic sense of entitlement, writes Sally Weintrobe (2012), her voice crying in the wilderness, prevents us from emerging from our comfortable fog of doublethink.

By double-mindedness, however, I mean something much more problematic than mere denial. Double-minded, we live in two realities at once. We know about the climate crisis, and perhaps even that it is rapidly becoming dire. But in a mental gesture akin to throwing up our hands, we say, this is too big for me or for any individual. Only systemic changes matter. So we go on working with our patients and our psychoanalytic politics, as humanistically as we know how to work, while our common home becomes a burning world (Cushman, 2007). Essentially, we, like Freud in the 1930s, and like the millions of "ordinary Germans" in the period studied by Thomas Kohut (T. A. Kohut, 2012) and others, have disabled the fire alarm. To accomplish this, as we shall see, we have taught ourselves not to see those worst affected as human just like ourselves, as others whose suffering matters.

We could spend chapters, articles, and books asking how this happens. A vast literature on multiple types of dissociation (Bromberg, 2006; Chefetz, 2000; Herman, 2009, 2011; Howell & Itzkowitz, 2016) and Freudian repression (Brenner, 1962; Jacobson, 1957; Loewald, 1955; Volkan, 1994) is now available to us. More immediately useful might be to ask how, faced with crisis, we, living daily in our professional minds with these concepts, might emerge rapidly to protect our common home. Will our theories help us enough—surely they have not until now—or do we need something else to shake us out of our analytic slumbers? Speaking to psychoanalysts, who often characterize ourselves not as belonging to the STEM (science, technology, engineering, mathematics) disciplines but to the tellers of stories, philosopher Judith Butler (2005) writes:

> But what if the narrative reconstruction of a life *cannot* be the goal of psychoanalysis, and that the reason for this has to do with the very formation of the subject? If the other is always there, from the start, in the place where the ego will be, then a life is constituted through a fundamental interruption, is even *interrupted prior to the possibility of any continuity.*
>
> (p. 52)[7]

My guess is that we cannot see, cannot feel this prior interruption of the other, primarily because we are so embedded in the cultures that have created the climate problem. As many have noted, Freud grew up intellectually in, and was deeply attached to, the Enlightenment and Romantic European culture that enshrined individual autonomy as the ultimate good. We psychoanalysts have inherited his deep assumptions, along with a certain blindness to threats to the "common good," an ancient stoic and medieval notion that went missing in the modern and Enlightenment period. Additionally, attached to these cultures in part because of the traumatic background of contemporary psychoanalysis (T. Kohut, 2003; Kuriloff, 2014) creating a desperate need for home, we may have forgotten the other destitute homeless of the world, in particular of the Southern Hemisphere. We need a contextualist analysis of our doublemindedness, and a radical ethic to shake us out of it.

Of course there are many contexts we could consider—historical, religious, scientific—but for now, let us think of the emotional.

Sources of evasion I: fear of vulnerability

What produces our dissociative evasion of the magnitude of climate crisis? As suggested in Chapter 1, the general egoism and hyper-entitlement of Western culture in the industrial era has protected us from caring about those most affected. Chapter 2 surmised that the unconscious ghosts of colonialism, slavery, and racism keep us even from seeing the Global south and its suffering. Even closer, though, we find ourselves out of touch with our own vulnerability, shared with all mortal creatures, and, we now realize, with the earth itself as an interconnected living ecosystem. Though a few lonely philosophical voices—Socrates, Marcus Aurelius, Montaigne—have always taught us to live daily aware of death (Critchley, 2009), our counterphobic, masculinist, dominant and dominating culture has improvised science, technology, and especially technological medicine to hide this impending reality from us. Even religion conspires by placing modern churches far from graveyards. Psychoanalysis in its Kleinian forms holds that we are torn between a life instinct and a death instinct, carefully disguised from ourselves. Johannes Brahms, on the contrary, in his *Deutsches Requiem*, reminds us for 80 minutes that "all flesh is like grass, and all human glory like flowers which wither and fall away." The baritone sings out, "Lord, teach me that my end comes, and that my life has a measure, so that I must leave it." We have the cultural resources, often well-known to well-educated psychoanalysts, to help us embrace our vulnerability so that we may respond, not simply react.

Vulnerability, however, takes many forms short of death, or rather, besides death. Thinking of Antigone and of Hector, we remember that the Greeks already realized that the dead remain defenseless against desecration, needing protection and reverence (Woodruff, 2014). Susceptible to illness, injury, and disability, we may either take up extreme sports, build medical bunkers, or carry extreme insurance. In fear of poverty, we may spend our lives accumulating wealth. Whatever vulnerability we saw in our parents may be our greatest fear, the one we determine to protect against. To protect ourselves from every possible harm, we may become either gun-toting bigots or quietly guarded protectors of what we believe to be ours. Of course variations abound. We psychoanalysts can write tomes about the many forms that self-protectiveness against expe-riential vulnerabilities can take. Working to bring people out from these private fearful worlds into connection with actual others as Fairbairn wrote long ago (Fairbairn, 1952), we psychoanalysts and other psychotherapists devote our lives.

And yet, our fear of vulnerability runs very deep, further rooted, I believe in many kinds of shame, a preoccupation of many "sha-meniks" of various psychoanalytic persuasions (Buechler, 2008; DeYoung, 2015; M. R. Lansky & Morrison, 1997; A. P. Morrison, 1996; Orange, 2008; L. Wurmser, 1991) since Helen Block Lewis (H. B. Lewis, 1974) and Heinz Kohut (H. Kohut, 1971, 1977) both foregrounded it in the early 1970s. Let us consider shame, as well as its backside envy, both to uncover its function in generating the climate crisis as well as to see how it acts so dangerously in keeping us bystanders.

Sources of evasion 2: shame and fear of responsibility

Of course my first thought when I need to write about shame is that I will have nothing intelligent to say, and that you will be dis-appointed. Just as my mother said, I am worthless, lazy, good-for-nothing, and selfish, and you will wish you had not given up your precious time to read such a boring blockhead. Shame never quits. But since shame may be keeping us paralyzed in the face of climate change, let us go on anyway. Actually it may seem unnecessary to define shame, 35 years after Lewis and Kohut brought it center stage in psychoanalytic theory and practice, and have shown us how insidiously and unconsciously shame infects our lives. But what is most familiar can also be most difficult to see, embedded as we are.

What is shame?[8] The pioneers in the study of shame—Leon Wur-mser in the classical tradition, Francis Broucek from developmental and emotion studies, and especially Andrew Morrison in self psychology—have sensitized us to shame's pervasiveness in human life and to its disastrous effects, from underachievement and depression to self-hatred and suicide in individual lives, to war, rape, and torture in societal contexts. They have studied its origins, and its many manifestations. Andy Morrison, directly and indirectly the teacher of so many of us, in particular showed how integral shame is to the forms of narcissism studied by early self psychologists, and how much the understanding of shame contributes to the treatment of the afflicted ones. Shame he saw as "an affect reflecting a sense of failure or deficit of the self" (A. Morrison, 1984), as opposed to guilt over what we have done, and for which we owe restitution.

But let us consider other definitions, and instead of choosing among them, let us suppose that they each grasp an aspect of what we mean by the word. The careful reader will note, however, subtle differences in emphasis between those who see shame primarily as an individual affect, and those who see it as an emergent property of an emotional system. Here is Lansky's (M. Lansky, 1999) definition, including his very useful distinction between shame and guilt:

> Shame is about the self. The word as we now understand it refers, not simply to one type of affect, but to a complex emotional system regulating the social bond, that is signaling disturbance to the status of the self within the social order: what is one is before oneself and others; one's standing, importance, or lack of it; one's lovability, sense of acceptability, or imminent rejection, as seen before the eye of the other or the internal self-evaluative eye of the self. This essential relationship to the self is in contrast to the domain of guilt, which does not concern the self—what one is—so much as it does what one does—real or fantasied actions, transgressions, or omissions that harm the other.
>
> (p. 347)

My own thesis, as you might expect from me (Orange, 1995; Orange et al., 1997), is that shame in the psychoanalytic system belongs neither to the patient nor to the analyst, but is intersubjectively generated, maintained, exacerbated, and we hope, mitigated, within the relational system. Likewise, shame, hiding our vulnerability and inadequacies in the face of climate change, emerges intersubjectively. No one is born ashamed, but, paralyzed, we can surely inhabit together experiential worlds of what an American writer of the 1930s Great Depression called "that ratty gnawing shame."

Morrison (A. P. Morrison, 1984) has taught us that the psychoanalyst must be ready to notice both shame and shame-anxiety:

> recognition and acceptance of the patient's shame lies at the heart of empathic listening in the analytic process . . . it must also be remembered that shame itself, as well as the material that causes it, will frequently be hidden and withdrawn from the analyst, particularly by the patient with narcissistic pathology. It must be sought actively and with patience by the respectful analyst-selfobject,[9] "teased out," particularly from the narcissistic rage[10] of the vulnerable, self-impaired individual.
>
> (p. 501)

The study of shame, however, has often been embedded in assumptions that many of us no longer share: first, that emotions are really physical somethings called "affects," a term that lends itself, in my view, to reification and to neuroistic (Brothers, 2001) reductionism. Second, these "affects" are considered single, atomistic mental states characterized by recognizable physiological manifestations. They are, third, most often thought to belong primarily or exclusively to those single individuals that my collaborators and I have called isolated minds. In other words, the study of shame long lived within the egoistic monism described in our first chapter.

For affect theorist Sylvan Tomkins (Tomkins, 1962–3), for example, shame was defined as a slumping posture with drooping head and looking aside, seen quite early in infancy. He considered it a hardwired response to interest interruptions, independent of relational experience. "Shame is inevitable for any human being insofar as desire outruns fulfillment sufficiently to attenuate interest without destroying it" (p. 185). Michael Lewis (M. Lewis, 1992), a researcher on cognitive and affective development, sees shame as a later development, dependent on the child's development of conscious self-awareness and a sense of being viewed. Shame also requires a sense of success and failure in regard to standards and rules, and is equivalent to a global sense of failure. In neither theorist do we find much reference to the person's experience or to the relational context.

Others, however, have begun to study emotional life differently. Lichtenberg, whose motivational systems theory (Lichtenberg, Lachmann, & Fosshage, 1992, 1996, 2002) attempts to map the general contours of a person's emotional life, comments with respect to Tomkins's account of shame—also adopted by Broucek (Broucek, 1991)—that he prefers: "a theory that regards the baby during the first year as having a spectrum of aversive affects, one of which is an experience that lies in continuity with what is later more easily categorized as shame" (Lichtenberg, 1994, pp. 126–127). This approach, though it retains the affect idea, is more relational— "aversive" implies turning from something or someone—and is also far more systemic and less concrete.

Recently, however, theorists inspired by systems, chaos, and complexity theories (Beebe & Lachmann, 2002; Coburn, 2014; Fogel, 1993; Sander, 1982; Stolorow, Atwood, & Orange, 2002) have pointed the way toward an even more radical rethinking of shame in psychoanalysis. Despite important differences among these theorists, these thinkers have not only questioned and rethought the sharp distinctions usually assumed between cognition and affect, or as I would prefer to say, between thought and emotional life. Even more important, these theorists have regarded emotion as an emergent property of relational systems, as the total embodied involvement and participation in such intersubjective fields. Sander (1982), for example, taught us to regard the infant, caregiver, and interactions between them as making up a system including every aspect of development. Fogel (1993) has made the shift from affect to emotion, seeing emotion as one form of embodied cognition/participation in organic systems or cultures. Beebe and Lachmann (2002) have drawn our attention to the fine points of self-and-mutual regulation, showing us how emotional participation in dialogic systems works in detail. Our own work (Stolorow et al., 2002) has steadfastly refused the cognition–emotion dichotomy, and claimed that psychoanalytic understanding of experiential worlds, yours, mine, and ours, constitutes decisive evidence against this dualism.

Even in the experiential worlds of shame, which feel so aversive and isolating, we are intricately involved in intersubjective systems and in worlds of complexity. By an intersubjective system I mean "any psychological field formed by interacting worlds of experience, at whatever developmental level these may be organized" (Stolorow & Atwood, 1992). In an intersubjective shame system, we feel we are deficient by comparison with the others (envy), we feel we are failures in our own and others' eyes, we feel so held up to critical scrutiny in our desperate misery that we want to sink into the ground and become invisible. From our wretched hell, we feel like the shades being stared at by Dante, who is reproached by Alessio Interminei: "Why are you so greedy to look at me when all of these are just as filthy?" (Alighieri, 1994). Later Virgil asks him: "What are you staring at? Why let your vision linger there down among the disconsolate and mutilated shades?" (Canto XXIX). Dante in turn is ashamed before Virgil, who has seen his "drunken eyes."[11]

Philosophers, too, have taken an interest in shame, especially noting that it seems to have useful functions in human life as well as the disastrous ones alluded to above. It is no compliment to call someone "shameless."[12] Martha Nussbaum (Nussbaum, 2004), particularly drawing on the work of Winnicott for her developmental ideas, argues that shame originates from the awareness of one's vulnerabilities in the presence of others. Although the capacity to feel shame may have important social benefits, she thinks that the harm generated by shaming makes it immoral to use it for punishment. (We might, strategically, ask how useful or counterproductive shaming may be for addressing climate change.) Anxiety about shame, she believes, creates societal systems that value strength over vulnerability, encouraging men especially to embrace a rigid self-ideal of independence and invulnerability. To many of us, solidarity means vulnerability to feeling the suffering of others, suffering that we cause, as in climate change and economic exploitation. Perhaps we need to reconsider both the profound destructiveness of shame, and our central need for it.

British moral philosopher Bernard Williams has captured much of the phenomenological experience of shame, and of its relational embeddedness:

> in the experience of shame, one's whole being seems diminished or lessened. In my experience of shame, the other sees all of me and all through me, even if the occasion of shame is on my surface—for instance, in my appearance; and the expression of shame, in general, as well as in the particular form of it that is embarrassment, is not just the desire to hide, or to hide my face, but the desire to disappear, not to be there. It is not even the wish, as people say, to sink through the floor, but rather the wish that the space occupied by me should be instantaneously empty.
> (Williams, 1993, p. 89)

Consider the situation, for example, of a woman whose husband or romantic partner has continued his attachment to his previous partner but is ashamed to say so. To guard the bond between them, she has needed to believe his claims that the previous relationship is finished, and that she could finally keep him and get him to love her as she desperately needs to be loved. They live within a world of shame. When the evidence confounds her, she becomes full of preoccupation with suicide. We can understand this both as her rage against herself for being duped, and against him for using her, but also, as Williams says, as a desire "that the relational space occupied by me should be empty." She cannot bear that anyone should even look at her, she feels so degraded. And unfortunately, her fear of this feeling kept her from looking clearly at her situation in the first place.

Or consider this story from *The New York Times* about Qingming, a Chinese peasant from an abjectly poor family. To attend college, he had to pass the entrance test. But each student had to finish paying all fees first, the teacher repeated, and Qingming, $80 short, stood up before all, in shame and anger:

> "I do not have the money," he said slowly, according to several teachers who described the events that morning. But his teacher—and the system—would not budge.
>
> A few hours later, Qingming, 18 years old, stepped in front of an approaching locomotive. (August 1, 2004).
>
> (Kahn & Yardley, 2004)

Here we can see that shame is neither affect nor cognition. Nor does it belong primarily or exclusively to Qingming. Rather an emergent shame-process pervaded an entire experiential world. Qingming's shame-ridden world included his family, his school, his changing and traditional culture, his hopes and possibilities, his rage and despair. As Williams suggests, he could no longer inhabit this world of rage and shame, or allow it to inhabit him. Absent a compassionate witness, the shame-system destroyed him.

This example leads us to the relationship between humiliation and shame, sometimes described as two different affects. Some instead see humiliation as a form of shame. My preference would be to regard humiliation as the intersubjective process most often involved in creating experiential worlds of shame. Forms of humiliation, of course, range from early shaming parent–child interactions, through bullying in contexts like school and work, into rape, enslavement, and torture. Each of these establishes a shaming system, in which the dominator tries to overcome shame, "the underside of narcissism" (A. Morrison, 1989) by humiliating the other, that is, by shaming her or him. Some have speculated that empathy is possible because we are prewired to, or have the capacity to, experience both sides of exchanges. This could mean that we are born prepared to participate in relational systems, including those organized primarily around shame. Kilborne (Kilborne, 2008) also rightly notes that massive parental unresponsiveness can lead to shame and envy, by way of profound convictions of unlovability.[13] Does the grip of such convictions keep us blind to the suffering of others, in which we are so systematically involved? (Shame and envy may prevent us from feeling climate injustice.)

A further aspect of shame that makes it worth considering as a systems concept rather than as an affect in an individual is its pervasive quality. In Morrison's evocative words, "shame settles in like a dense fog, obscuring everything else, imposing only its own shapeless, substanceless impression. It becomes impossible to establish bearings or to orient oneself in relation to the broader landscape" (A. Morrison, 1994). Like an invasive weed or a computer virus, it tends to insinuate itself into my whole life, my whole experiential world, and to spoil everything. I did not simply fail to complete the marathon; rather, *I am a failure*. I did not just inadvertently retraumatize my patient; I *am* a failure as an analyst, and thus as a human being. I did not only complain about my sore feet; I *am* simply a selfish person. This pervasive quality of shame, of course, suggests its origins in the family, where my own experiential world became organized around a sense of myself as worthless, good-for-nothing, and selfish. Worst of all, there is no hope of escape from the enclosure of this world except through the encounter with another with whom I must again enter worlds of shame.

Climate shame similarly paralyzes. If every time I drive to my doctor's office, I take on the carbon debt of the whole developed world, I may become unable to think creatively about what I, or we together, can do to make a difference. Likewise, a pervasive culture of shame, like the microcultures we encounter in psychoanalytically informed therapies, leads many of us to lives of greed and envy, perhaps the major inhibitor in our struggle to consider the radical changes needed to turn back the climate emergency so quickly engulfing us. Let us now consider envy, the crucial link between widespread shame and the predicament in which we find ourselves.

Envy

Envy, a crucial factor in the hyper-consumption so central to the climate crisis, has been a neglected emotion in contemporary psychoanalysis, despite—or perhaps because of—its prominence in the penis envy Freud (Freud & Riviere, 1922) attributed to all women, and as prominent manifestation of Kleinian (Klein, 1957) aggression. For those who have rejected instinct theories and consider relationality as foundational in human life generally and in psychotherapy in particular, envy has fallen out of sight. We might ask why.

Philosophers have tended to consider envy simply as the desire for what the other possesses, though often it comes combined with wishing harm to the other who has what we desire. Some argue about whether to consider envy morally reprehensible; Spinoza, for example, considered it simply part of human nature. We naturally pity those less fortunate, and envy those more fortunate,[14] he thought (Spinoza & Parkinson, 2000). Some philosophers see envy simply as a less interesting form of jealousy, a more complex and more obviously relational emotion. We are jealous in relation to people; we are envious in relation to possessions or status. Nevertheless, notes British moral philosopher Peter Goldie, "envy is not just non-relatively wanting more of something; it is wanting more of that *than* someone else" (Goldie, 2000, p. 221). Moreover, he notes, envy tells us something very important about ourselves: "What I envy will, to some extent, reflect what I value" (p. 221). This seems to me a point worth reflecting on. Personally, I don't envy celebrity, great wealth, outrageous beauty, or tremendous cleverness. I do envy depth of learning and scholarship, great musicianship, a sense of style, generosity and compassion, practical wisdom, and the capacity to play tennis. What I envy tells you and me much about who I am.

In many cultures, especially those of the Mediterranean and Middle East, envy plays a central explanatory role in human communities under the rubric of the "evil eye" (Aquaro, 2004; Kilborne, 2008; Wurmser & Jarass, 2008), where almost every untoward event can be traced to envy. In these cultures, if someone falls ill, it happened because someone envied him or her. The younger and more vulnerable need special protection from the envious "evil eye," the envy that can kill by looking. Each culture has its forms of protection against envy—to outsiders, these are superstitions. These forms may be simple or elaborate: gestures, spitting, incantations. In many places in Italy, it is still customary to ward off the evil eye by responding to any good fortune or any compliment by saying "*Si mal occhio non ci fosse*" (untranslatable, but "that the evil eye may not come") more or less as English speakers might say "knock on wood," as if commenting on good fortune or praising someone or something were truly dangerous.[15] In the Downton Abbey world, people repeat "Bad harvest! Bad harvest!" We dare not brag or expose ourselves to the envious, who, like us, might want to destroy those who possess what they envy. Kilborne (Kilborne, 2008) reports that among the Souss of Morocco, a victim of envy was directed by the wise woman to wash a talisman in water until the markings were dissolved, "then to pour this water over a piece of red-hot iron heated in red-hot coals" (p. 133). The color red is considered protective against the evil eye in many of these cultures. In general, it is considered wise to keep a low profile and not to seem important or wealthy. Where children in the United States want to grow up to be celebrities, in many cultures a suspicion exists that being a somebody can be dangerous. "Don't be a tall poppy," Australians warn, "you will get cut down." Envy, with its deadly perils, lurks everywhere. Not a Kleinian instinct, but a universal human potential ready to strike anywhere and everywhere, it threatens the unwary. It prepares us to "grab . . . all the nourishment, air and sun" (Levinas, 1990, p. 100), becoming usurpers and murderers.

So why has envy disappeared from our Anglophone cultural and psychoanalytic discourse? Anthropologists (Schoeck, 1987), theologians (Aquaro, 2004), and psychoanalysts (Kilborne, 2008) speculate that the rags-to-riches tale of Horatio Alger has fused with democratic aspirations to make envy disappear in our cultures. Instead of casting the evil eye, we work longer and longer hours, consuming and consuming, in order to keep up with the Joneses.

We no longer worry about conspicuous consumption that in other cultures would attract violence. Driving luxury cars or living in palaces when our neighbors perhaps only blocks away live in direst poverty has become ordinary to us. Our cultural myths tell us that everyone can have what we have if they work as hard as we have done. Convinced that we are somebodies because we deserve to be, and they are nobodies because they deserve to be, we are shocked when violence comes to our centers of finance and leisure. What do they have against us, we wonder? We begin to speculate that certain religions encourage violence. We have forgotten envy and shame. Shame has become "low self-esteem," a much less degraded-sounding condition. But I am getting ahead of my story. I do not agree with the anthropologists that envy has disappeared from our cultures, but rather that we have developed massive cultural defenses against acknowledging it. I believe that the very cultural myths that hide envy from our view—that every individual can climb out of poverty and have as much as everyone else, and that my wealth does not disadvantage anyone—are based on the avoidance of shame. The same mentality hides from us the consequences of our carbon-and-methane, oil and beef, lives.

Instead of a shame-and-envy culture that requires us to keep a very low profile, we have developed what former Oberlin College president Robert Fuller (Fuller, 2003) calls a culture of "rankism," in which we avoid shame by constantly measuring our rank, and doing everything in our power to increase it. Of course this can come only at the expense of others. Envy, as psychoanalysts Morrison and Lansky (A. Morrison & Lansky, 2008) also note, feeds on comparison. To become a somebody in such a system, I have to make you a nobody, often by having more and larger houses or driving more expensive cars. Envious rankism drives compulsive consumption. Fuller's inspiring book, *All Rise: Somebodies, Nobodies, and the Politics of Dignity* (Fuller, 2006), imagines a world in which envy could be transformed into profound respect through reforming institutions.

But, if envy is part of our human nature, perhaps built into nat-ural selection (Boris, 1994), can we transform it? Is it a normal

developmental process that can either support developmental striving, or turn harmful or deadly? Can therapeutic work change its
malignant forms or harness its energy for, as Freud would have said,
sublimation? To answer these questions, we must look a bit more
closely, both theoretically and clinically.

On the theoretical side, I do not believe envy is a thing in itself,
but rather a process. This means, it cannot be quantified. Second,
I believe it is a relational process, not a process that belongs to one
person, to a patient, an analyst, or to a single one of us double-
minded about the climate crisis. Envy, in my view, arises in a specific
intersubjective field or system as a byproduct of shame, shame that
itself is already or ongoingly intersubjectively configured in worlds
of humiliation and deprivation and/or contempt. Note that I do
not say that envy is a defense against shame. It could be in some
instances,[16] but I do not think this belongs to its essential character, but that the relationship is much closer. Envy manifests the
shame itself. I envy you precisely because I feel so degraded and
inadequate. If I felt that I fully belonged in the human community,
I would not be interested in what you have, except to rejoice with
you. Much less would I be involved in envy's first cousin, *Schaden-
freude*, taking pleasure in your pain, if I were contented with what I
am and have. But further, I envy precisely you, and in this specific
"joint situation," to use Staemmler's (2012) useful expression. I am
less envious, and less ashamed, with persons who welcome me as a
fellow human in the spirit of respect long championed by pioneers
like Frieda Fromm-Reichmann (Fromm-Reichmann, 1950) and
Sandor Ferenczi.

So when patients envy the possessions, relationships, recognition,
or even the good health of others, I often listen for what they are
implicitly saying about their own inadequacies. What sounds like
hatred of the others, turns out to be self-loathing or shame. Humiliated, we need to hide from the other's judgmental and envious
looking: envious, we become the other whose looks can kill. But I
also ask myself what my patients are picking up from the relational
context, both in their outside worlds and with me, that contributes

to and exacerbates the shame and envy experiences. Here is a small clinical story.

My patient Ted, a professor at Columbia University who had also attended there as an undergraduate and graduate student, came to me depressed and anxious about finishing the book he needed to have published before his tenure review. He knew he had the ability, and the most eminent scholars in his field respected and supported him, but he was stuck, never feeling that he had read enough, or "covered all the bases." He knew of my academic background, and had heard that I *had* finished a book, and hoped I might be able to help him. He was also very much concerned that he had not been able to marry and establish a family, apparently always choosing the wrong partners, and feared that something might be irredeemably wrong with him.

We worked for several years, during which he concluded that he was stuck because he really didn't want to be a professor, but had been blindly following others' agenda for him, and found his way into another line of work that suited him very well. In addition, after years of work on his family's multiple forms of invalidation and shaming, he was able to find a partner and settle down.

Along the way, however, perhaps two years into a twice-weekly treatment, Ted began one day: "I've been thinking, and I'm trying to figure out why you hate Columbia. Yes, the university has hurt me, and yes, it has given me everything that my family couldn't give and didn't want me to have. But you are so supportive and encouraging to me, and yet there is this thing about Columbia. I've felt we're getting nowhere for some time now, and I wonder if it has something to do with this." Considerably surprised, and playing for time to respond, I asked him to tell me more. It seemed I had responded much more strongly to his complaints about than to his satisfaction with the university, and this for the whole length of the treatment.

I took a deep breath, and told him that I wasn't sure, but that I guessed that I had nothing against Columbia, but that I had grown up in a world where no one ever seemed to have heard of the Ivy League, and that no one had ever felt I was capable or worthy of a first-rate education. Now my colleagues and patients included many people with undergraduate degrees and doctorates from these first-rate places, as well as from Oxford and Cambridge. Often these people asked me where I had gone to college, and I had to answer: You will never have heard of it. And I was never wrong about this, but always painfully ashamed. I told him I was really sorry that my envy and shame had been hurting and confusing him. He seemed greatly relieved, telling me that he had felt that my reactions had been confirming his sense that something was terribly wrong with him for working in a terrible institution like Columbia University. We were soon very much back on track, and this became one of our shared jokes.

Again, this could seem to be an everyday garden-variety story of the analyst's envious shame. But let us look again. Yes, I bring to every interaction of my life an experiential world structured by my mother's shaming epithets: worthless, good-for-nothing, and selfish, as well as by my father's contempt and humiliating violence. I bring with me the potential to feel either mildly or desperately inadequate, like Pigpen's cloud of dust that precedes his arrival. But no, I don't hate Harvard, Yale, Princeton, Columbia, Oxford, or Cambridge, and they come into the foreground of my dialogic-self-awareness only in specific relational contexts. The contexts themselves may or may not be shame-makers—it depends. Similarly, I find that patients who grew up with trust funds—often ashamed themselves of their privileged lives in relation to me—can evoke shame between us that does not seem to have preexisted the encounter. My experiences with such patients, and theirs with me, have been so varied that I cannot help thinking of shame as a quality of a particular and vulnerable emotional world in which we participate together.

Climate shame, I believe, takes two principal forms: (1) the fear of visible vulnerability that keeps us indifferent to the nature and extent of the crisis; and (2) continuing envy of those who have more, so that those deprived of essential needs become invisible. In our striving we reach for more space, larger houses and cars, more things, perfect bodies that resist growing or appearing old. Entangled together, these two aspects of shame feed self-enclosed preoccupation, utterly distracting us from the descriptions and warnings of the best climate science. The first, the fear of vulnerability, akin to what Robbert Wille calls "the shame of existing" (Wille, 2014), keeps us self-protective and enclosed, endangering us humans, other species, and our planetary home. Without the fundamental experience of being held and cherished, we lack the emotional sense of belonging among other humans, or anywhere. Thus we treat our world, and implicitly ourselves, like disposable garbage. The second, envy, attempts to restore an ersatz well-being, to cover up the rotten sense of shame with fame, money, and glamour. Any sense that others have more occludes our ethical vision, blinding us to our involvement in injustice and deafening us to the cries of those we are harming every day. Much less can we, envious of those who have more, notice that we in the "first world" live as beneficiaries of massive injustices perpetrated by our colonialist ancestors on the indigenous "first peoples" in the Americas, Australia, New Zealand, and elsewhere, as well as on prosperity originally created by systems of human bondage also called slavery (see Chapter 2). For this unconsciousness to fade, or better said, to wake up morally, we would need that indispensable and painful moral form of shame, awareness of our implication in systems of evil, to replace the shame and envy that traps us in compulsive consuming.

Just as psychoanalytic treatment of shame begins to restore to the mistreated a sense of inclusion in the human community, so can a psychoanalytic sensibility, sensitive to the corrosive and isolating effects of shame, begin to link us all with each other. We can begin to understand that our well-being depends on the well-being of others, and restore the old notion of the common good.

What we can offer (1): trauma, shame, and transformation

In our first chapter we noted that seeming indifference to the climate emergency often results from traumatic freezing or paralysis. Like the devastated patients we treat every day, we find ourselves overwhelmed by the magnitude of the crisis, and by the enormity of the power and money arrayed against those who want to turn a corner to keep our planet livable for all. Now we have considered the role of shame and envy both in generating the consumerist culture responsible for so much carbon production, and in keeping us from accepting our extreme vulnerability to the "extremely probable" outcomes. So we hide, as shame always bids us do, in our offices, in our doorman buildings and gated communities, and hope the tornadoes, hurricanes, droughts, and wildfires go somewhere else. Pretending invulnerability, ashamed that we are at risk and continue to place others at risk, we go on.

As clinicians, however, we have learned that naming what we fear, naming our secret shame, tends to increase solidarity. Having thought we were alone, we find others in the same boat. Gradually, we even learn that common vulnerability lessens the shame. If everyone in my club has only one leg, or one working ear, we can talk about what it is like to be the way we are, and speak together about common action. Coming out of the closet about climate vulnerability may bring us together in a common resolve that will surprise those with money and power so used to keeping us helpless and ashamed. As psychoanalysts begin to speak out, attend protests, engage in non-violent resistance, many others, both patients and analysts, will gain courage.[17] As Erik Erikson asked long ago: "Can we ever claim, either on our clinical homeground or in the border areas of wider application, to be merely healing our clients in offices and clinics and to be rationally enlightening our students and readers, without intervening—whether we avow it or not—in the processes by which values are formed and transmitted in our society?" (Erikson, 1976, p. 410). So, willy-nilly, like it or not, we are active or passive players in our larger worlds.

What we can offer (2): witness, holding, and active concern

Psychoanalysts bring to the ethical table long experience as witnesses to trauma and injustice, experience that equips us for some kinds of leadership in confronting the climate emergency. All day long we help people to name what they are feeling, especially their embodied experience, often of trouble that seems too big for any words they know, too big or too old for narrative, too terrible to hold in mind.

At times of horror, the witnessing function becomes crucial. Just recently I rediscovered something I had written in the days just after September 11, 2001, to my family, friends, and colleagues who lived far from New York, and who had contacted me to see whether I was safe:

> Yesterday for six hours, (and I will do it again today), I joined dozens of other licensed mental health professionals at a missing-persons hotline, organized by the Red Cross before the police and federal emergency management people had a chance to set up their much more comprehensive system for determining who is lost and for doing the DNA testing and so on. This hotline had received about 60,000 calls from family and friends of about 6,500 people who could not be found in the first two days. Each person was told that there would be a call back. We are doing the calling back. We try to reach the person who originally called, ask if they have learned anything, and ask if they can give us any more details about the person (our database is being merged with the big one, but no one calls people back from there, except FBI), and answer their questions (is there still any hope?, could a person who was in this place have escaped? . . .), mostly with "we don't really know." Mostly we listen to whatever they want to say, and find out whether they are alone or with other family members, and give them telephone numbers for whatever they need, especially including mental health services.
>
> Before I make each call, I read where the person worked (e.g. Windows on the World restaurant, or 93rd floor Tower 2, or 104th floor Tower 1, or at near ground level), because the conversation will be different because of that. If any details—height, weight, skin color, clothing—are already there, I try to imagine the person, and the caller, who may be wife, husband, parent,

cousin, friend. Many callers are far away from New York, and these are often the ones most grateful for my call, and wanting to talk about their last contact with the person, and what sort of person this was. Often I am writing down small personal details like what was written inside the wedding band (25 years), or what kind of surgical scar the person has/had. Some don't want to talk, and others do. But there is no good news for any of these people, except for one who had discovered that the person she had thought lost had really arrived later. Such an instance goes into an extremely small "found" pile. Most people understand almost immediately that there is no more information, and that now after 4–5 days, there is nothing to do but to grieve and to grieve. So that is what we are mostly doing with one person after another. And trying to comfort each other between calls.

For me and for others—and I should say that the psycho-analytic community has very much participated in the various mental health volunteer services—this is really so hard that we almost can't bear it. And yet it seems so important that when, last night, they begged me to sign up again for today, I couldn't just walk away. But the initial shock and fear has turned for me into something else that I really don't know how to describe, but that I sense is shared by many others. Even as parts of the city return to a creepy kind of normality, the experience becomes worse and worse.

All of you know that I don't normally write these group let-ters, because I really don't like them. But I wanted you to have a sense of my life in this disaster, life that feels more like death. It's hard to think philosophically, or politically, right now. I hope that you who have more distance can do that. For me, the visual image is always Picasso's Guernica (maybe they should send it back to New York now!), and the sound is Brahms' *German Requiem*.

Back to climate crisis, we psychoanalysts can use what we have learned about dissociation, denial, what I am calling double-mindedness, to refind our witnessing function. Witnessing the damage our consumerist lifestyles and worship of money are inflicting on our brothers and sisters both among us and in the Global South, we can restore awareness that, as climate activists love to say, everything is connected. We have learned from Bion (Bion, 1959) and from Hans Loewald (Loewald, 1960, 1970, 1972, 1979) to understand failures in linking as the source of most problematic unconsciousness, and restoration of linking as a crucial aspect of therapeutic action. Climate awareness, crisis consciousness, can help us to help our patients, ourselves, and each other to name and organize the disparate phenomena in our personal and communal worlds, and to say that this cannot go on. Once we have witnessed our common situation to this extent, we ask ourselves what each of us can do. What is possible for me at my age in my situation? A 100-year-old member of my retirement community, a retired social worker, organized our entire town of 35,000 people this past year to take back its water governance from the Golden State Water Authority ruling southern California. Another collects all the hearing-aid batteries to see them properly recycled. Others teach us composting while others collect food and toiletries for our local homeless people. All of us save every possible drop of water, and reuse everything we can. We can do something at any age, in any situation.

Why we should and must: human, first-world, and privileged

In this section I will argue that psychoanalysis as a profession, and psychoanalysts as individuals, need to make three significant changes to embrace the ethical turn in the face of the climate crisis: (1) from double-mindedness to single-mindedness; (2) from narcissism to community; and (3) from elitism to solidarity. I will close by making a few practical suggestions. Along the way I will be relying both on the sense of emergency laid out in Chapter 1, as well as anticipating the account of radical ethics in the chapter to come. This means taking as granted that the climate emergency and social justice are not only matters of political justice, but the responsibility of each of us. It has become a matter of life and death.

What would it mean to become single-minded about the climate crisis? Surely it would not make us into Johnny-one-notes who can think and speak about nothing else. To the contrary, it would mean a clear-minded understanding that its urgency links us to the struggles for justice among peoples worldwide, as we noted in our first chapter and as the new papal encyclical, *Laudato Si* (Catholic Church Pope [2013– : Francis], 2015) clearly believes. This focus would shake us out of our complacency and teach us that we have everything to learn from the indigenous peoples on whose devastation we in North America are still living, and whom the fossil fuel industry ever more threatens. It would tell us that converting to biofuels has taken millions of acres from food production, starving our sisters and brothers worldwide. Like substituting gas for oil, or nuclear for both, such solutions are too simple, though attractive because they demand so little from the already privileged. Examples multiply, showing that single-mindedness must be complexity-mindedness. Vern Visick notes that the new papal encyclical repeats 12 times that "everything is connected," and explains that freedom must then have positive content: "what justice requires in each of the relationships that constitute our lives" (Visick, 2015, p. 414). Complexity theories (Cilliers, 2007; Coburn, 2014) tell us not only that everything is connected, but also that small changes can make a big difference, for good or ill. Complexity theories further warn us about tipping points, such as the ones we have already passed, to rising sea-levels, volatile and extreme weather, melting of the polar ice and glaciers, as well as those to come if we do not turn radically away from fossil fuels in the next three to five years.

Single-mindedness, like wholeheartedness, has fueled the most important social, political, and ethical changes we can remember. British and U.S. abolitionism (Davis, 2006), the U.S. civil rights struggle, and the struggle against apartheid readily come to mind. All were grass-roots movements against racial aggression, with the support of individuals from the ruling classes but massively and violently resisted by established interests. Climate justice activists quickly point out that environmental pollution, from coal and other toxic waste, disproportionately affects people of color in North America as well as the global poor. As we noted in Chapter 2, climate injustice is racism, and racism creates the moral blindness involved in climate injustice. White-skinned people have grown wealthy from fossil fuels while making the earth uninhabitable for its black and brown inhabitants in the Southern Hemisphere, and for indigenous peoples everywhere. Instead, single-mindedly, embracing complexity, we must (Aron & Starr, 2012) beat the swords into plowshares and schools, where girls and boys can learn to build local communities that they control.

So a single-minded focus on our climate emergency will be inseparable from a renewed struggle for social justice, continuing the work of peace and justice left unfinished by Martin Luther King, whose voice for economic justice we still so badly need. For him:

> We as a nation must undergo a radical revolution of values. We must rapidly begin the shift from a "thing-oriented society" to a "person-oriented society." When machines and computers, profit motives and property rights, are considered more important than people, the giant triplets of racism, extreme materialism, and militarism are incapable of being conquered.
>
> ("Beyond Vietnam," www.commondreams.org/
> views04/0115-13.htm)

Pragmatically, each of us will need to concentrate efforts where we can, locally, regionally, nationally, worldwide. But understanding that all struggles for justice are connected means we need not worry that working primarily on racism or on education for girls in so-called developing countries means neglecting climate change, or vice versa. Instead, the question is, where can I make a difference right now? Keeping this question urgent will be the topic of our final chapter.

Second, the shift from narcissistic me-first entitlement to communitarian (some would say utopian) values will mean a deep conversion for much of first-world society. Many observers think it impossible, lamenting: "I really see no path to success on climate change. . . . No amount of psychological awareness will overcome people's reluctance to lower their standard of living" (Daniel Kahneman, quoted in Marshall, 2014, pp. 57–58). Oriented to a culture of celebrity, money, speed, and consumption, we scarcely interact with our neighbors. Even if, as Martin Luther King said, we occasionally act the Good Samaritan, throwing a coin to the street beggar, we rarely think through our participation in the unjust systems that create so many homeless. "If we do not act," proclaimed Dr. Martin Luther King, Jr., in Riverside Church in 1967, "we shall surely be dragged down the long, dark, and shameful corridors of time reserved for those who possess power without compassion, might without morality, and strength without sight" (King, 1986, p. 243). But King's name and voice are rarely heard in our psychoanalytic conferences, so we do not make the links.

Still, as Aron and Starr (Aron & Starr, 2012) write, psychoanalysis originally, before its entrenchment in psychiatry, oriented itself much more to the poor, and envisioned itself as a "psychotherapy for the people." What might this, in practical terms, mean? Besides the larger suggestion I advance below, we might consider some social class markers, of which my friend and colleague Elizabeth Corpt (2013) has written.

Corpt writes of class shame in psychoanalytic communities. Although her evocative descriptions of the experiences of such shame mean to add class to our ethical thinking about gender and race, the not-so-hidden question lurks: how and why do psychoanalytic institutes embody upper- and upper-middle-class elitism, making them inhospitable to working-class entrants? Historically, thanks to Aron and Starr (Aron & Starr, 2012), we understand that today's psychoanalysis inherited the medical hierarchy, keeping psychiatrists—the only acceptable applicants for psychoanalytic training in institutes of the American Psychoanalytic Association before the lawsuit resolved in the late 1980s required the admission of psychologists—in full control. Psychologists then stood above social workers and pastoral counselors, marriage and family counselors, and so on. Social workers, of course, were likely to be women. Even today, this hierarchy, though unofficial, persists in many psychoanalytic groups, making it more than difficult for the disadvantaged groups to feel equal as colleagues, but rather, as Corpt reports, like someone who does not know which fork to use, and feels a terrible sense of not belonging. I have added (Orange, 2013) that one may not even be able to afford the fork or the training, but that their advantages remain invisible to those who have them, like whiteness in the larger society (Jacobs, 2014).

Such hidden privilege, the legacy of summer camp and private schools, may isolate psychoanalysts, psychotherapists, and especially those in positions of leadership in training institutes from problems like climate justice, and our like-it-or-not involvement. Contemporary psychoanalytic theories, relational and intersubjective as they are, convince us of our inextricable presence in every clinical impasse or enactment, in every moment of every process with those sufferers whom we serve. With a few shining exceptions, these new theories have yet to touch our elitist isolation from the miserable lives of refugees from violence and abject poverty, from pervasive, continuing, and much-concealed violence against women, and from the devastation of our planet.

Elitism in every form resists change. A recent *New York Times* article (Lovett, 2015) described reactions in Los Angeles, famous and infamous for its love affair with and addiction to the internal combustion engine, "the city of fast cars and endless freeways," to proposals to increase bus and bicycle lanes, at the cost of some car lanes. Besides the fears of gridlock, two class issues enter the passionate discussion: cyclists (like this writer) are seen as minority elitists, and bus riders as minority impoverished folks who would not ride the bus if they could possibly afford a car. Who would want to join those people in a commute that requires waiting? According to one Angeleno, "I don't think most people out here are going to say, 'I'm going to take the bus,' unless getting in the car would just be madness." All the dispute concerned convenience and class issues; not one sentence related this question to climate change.

But suppose we psychoanalysts and other psychotherapists everywhere threw in our lot with those who have no choice, and rode buses, subways, and commuter trains as an eco-political act? Or, weather permitting, we could ride bicycles to work and play, saving our health as well as the planet. Yes, our patients may see us riding buses, subways, or bicycles, and wonder why. Changing our own patterns will naturally affect our clinical work. Without preaching, we change things, just as surely as if we sat down at the "wrong" end of a segregated bus. As Bernasconi (2006) writes, "there is no place for an ethical discourse that is not also inextricably linked with a recognition of the political context that it is its task to interrupt" (p. 256).

Low-carbon psychoanalysis

If the psychoanalytic community, not only as an aggregate of individual clinicians and scholars, but also as a public and organized body, becomes engaged with climate crisis, we can and should act decisively.

Following the model of the Tyndall Centre for Climate Change Research (tyndall.ac.uk/sites/default/files/twp161.pdf), we can face up to the carbon footprint of our professional and personal travel. The Tyndall Centre recognizes, as do we, the irreplaceable value of face-to-face discussions and relationships, but also the advantages for inclusiveness of digital communication. Neither they nor we can deny the extensive environmental damage done by flying. No one imagines that in the near future carbon-free fuels will run airplanes, so we must face up to this problem.

For the Tyndall researchers, trust and integrity are at stake. Until recently, they tell us shamefacedly, they have reported the carbon effects of flying and other means of transport, while flying around the world to conferences on climate change, accumulating frequent-flyer miles. But once we psychoanalysts take in their message, we too have an integrity problem. What are we, individually and collectively, to do?

As individuals, we can, of course, stop attending conferences that we cannot reach by train, short drives, bicycle, or walking. But that would seriously isolate many of us, and make only a minor impact, unless we wrote about our reasons. Collectively, we could do much more, setting an example for other professional and academic groups, as the Tyndall Centre is doing for us. We could:

1. Immediately join all psychoanalytic organizations worldwide into a Psychoanalytic Consortium, within which the historical groups could maintain their own sub-organizations and communications.
2. These sub-groups would agree, however, not to hold meetings to which members would fly, and would encourage inter-group membership and communication. Gradually, in the interest of common purposes, the lines between groups might become blurred, undoing the divisiveness Freud left us.
3. Building on the seminars and colloquia several psychoanalytic organizations like IARPP and IAPSP are already successfully holding online, we can converse with each other, develop new forms of education and training, include colleagues from far-flung parts of the world, without contributing to the rapidly worsening climate crisis. Video conferencing will reduce the sense of relational cost.
4. We can mitigate the losses we will suffer in immediate contacts with beloved colleagues by holding one huge and long conference every other summer in an otherwise empty college or university so that less affluent colleagues will not be priced out. All the traditional groups will meet within this space. We will break the image of psychoanalysis as elitist, becoming instead leaders in creating a new and responsible world that lives more simply and justly.
5. Someone who shares this vision, and with more organizational capacities than I possess, will need to reach out to the leaders of all the traditional psychoanalytic organizations immediately, to persuade them that it is past time to turn this corner, and to enlist them in doing it.

6. The most technologically capable and generous members of all groups will start study groups, seminars, colloquia, Internet meetings, and teach their local colleagues to use them. We will thus become leaders, not laggards, in the turn to low-carbon living.

7. Every psychoanalyst radically committed to addressing the climate crisis will write to her/his organizations about the reasons for flying-no-longer to conferences.

When I speak of these ideas with colleagues at home and overseas, the focus on climate crisis immediately disappears. Instead, I hear fears of being once again dominated by the IPA, of needing to work with colleagues from other organizations who have said hurtful and disparaging things. "It's too late," they say, to work together, to yield their hard-won gains for contemporary psychoanalysts to teach and train and hold their own conferences. I imagine that representatives of small, former colonial nations feel similarly at the U.N. and at the climate change conferences. Joining together, however, they may prevent wars, or find some recourse against the dominant nations. But if my idea is really impossible, what do my colleagues propose instead?

Psychoanalysts of all persuasions, for the moment, remaining caught in their old disputes, may renege on the responsibility their professional capabilities create in this moment. Our next chapter explains why, as individuals, we may not evade this crisis, even if our professional groups duck their heads.

Thomas A. Kohut, historian of the German psyche during the Nazi period, writes about our work:

> The consulting room does not exist in isolation but is inherently part of the world. Becoming more conscious of the connection between the consulting room and the world will not only have clinical and cultural benefits, but it will also enable psychoanalysis to assume its rightful place among the human sciences, studying the flow of history through psychological human beings.
>
> (T. Kohut, 2003, p. 236)

We must add, with other more famous thinkers, that our job now must be not only to study the grim reality our profligacy has created, but like prodigal sons and daughters, to repent, and to change what we have come to understand.

Notes

1. In a notable counterexample, Hanna Segal (1987b) urgently challenged the nuclear arms race: "While it is true that the nuclear arms race is not the only problem which afflicts our society, it is the one we cannot afford to postpone until other matters have been dealt with. Reversing the arms race, mobilizing public opinion so as to make it unacceptable, is the first step" (pp. 141–142). Elsewhere she interpreted, in good Kleinian style, nuclear weapons as manifestations of paranoid-schizoid thinking.
2. Two weeks after the appearance of the shocking Hoffman report, detailing the involvement of psychologists, and the organizational cover-up and collusion, Division 39, the psychoanalytic division of APA, carries not one word about these events on its webpage.
3. Bystandership, and the justification of others' suffering, constitute, I have argued (Orange, 2016), the content of the problem of evil. See also Bernstein (2002) and Segal (1987a).
4. Some (Ratzel, 1966) have observed that U.S. "Manifest Destiny," with its purposeful genocide of native peoples, was closely parallel to Hitler's *Lebensraum*, even the basis for it, but I cannot pursue this topic here.
5. From both psychological and ethical vantage points, it bears noting that such mobilization responded not to genocide but to threats to "homeland security," as we might say today.
6. A welcome exception appears in the not-yet-published work of Anthony Rankin Wilson, a Canadian musician and psychoanalyst who argues that we *must* (emphasis) reformulate our concept of self to include the world with which we are continuous if we are to have any chance to meet the challenge.
7. Writing of both Levinas and of Jean Laplanche, she continues: "To understand the unconscious . . . is to understand what *cannot* belong, properly speaking, to me, precisely because it defies the rhetoric of belonging, is a way of being dispossessed through the address of the other from the start" (p. 54).
8. Parts of this section are revised from Orange (2008) and used with permission.
9. "Selfobject," a technical term in psychoanalytic self psychology, refers to the person or function who supports the cohesion, continuity, and positive valuation of another's sense of self.
10. "Narcissistic rage," another technical term in psychoanalysis, refers to fury generated by a sense of insult to a person's fragile sense of self.
11. It may be of interest that shame is so often associated with the eyes, and that self-respect often seems so visible.
12. In my most recent work (Orange, 2016) I have considered Primo Levi's (1988) view of one kind of shame as indispensable to human beings: the awareness of the enormous, even infinite pain we are capable of inflicting on each other.

We privileged people may also need this kind of shame if we are to take on our responsibility for the climate emergency's effects on our most fragile brothers and sisters.

13. "Nonresponse, often organized around eyes that do not see, leads to an experience of soul blindness on the part of those on whom one depends for faith in human connections. This experience, in turns, makes one dependent on those who cannot see, and therefore who cannot see the one looking to them for response (linking blindness and nonresponse to shame). Such disorientation leads at once to hiding and rage at not being able to find the person looking, which then makes the looks of the disoriented that much more threatening to them. Envy then steps in to provide an orientation and defense against feelings of disorientation and disconnection, both sources of shame" (Kilborne, 2008, p. 146).

14. Similarly, Aristotle: "Envy is pain at the good fortune of others" *Rhetoric, Bk II,* Ch. 10 (Aristotle & McKeon, 1941).

15. Donald A. Braue reminds me that envy is fourth in rank among the seven deadly sins, and gets the most extensive treatment in the tenth biblical commandment. Interestingly, Dante's *Purgatorio* graduates envy to second after pride, and gives it three full cantos. Perhaps he thought that like pride, envy refuses reverence and gratitude, and thus more directly insults God than do the others, more aspects of human weakness. Our reading of envy as shame-based might challenge Dante's harsh judgment while still seeing envy's destructive effects for social justice.

16. This also depends on what theory of defense one holds (Brandchaft, Doctors, & Sorter, 2010; Orange, 2010).

17. As I write this, the news comes in that psychologists protected and implemented the U.S. torture program. It is long past time for us psychoanalysts, especially we who are also psychologists, to begin calling each other out. First coming out about our own ethical worries and climate vulnerability, we can then ask each other "Are you too your other's keeper?" Just as in the abolitionist era, and again with civil rights, we can summon each other to justice.

References

Alighieri, D. (1994). *The inferno* (R. Pinsky, Trans.). New York: Farrar, Straus and Giroux.

Aquaro, G. (2004). *Death by envy: The evil eye and envy in the Christian tradition.* New York: iUniverse.

Aristotle, & McKeon, R. (1941). *The basic works of Aristotle.* New York: Random House.

Aron, L., & Starr, K. E. (2012). *A psychotherapy for the people: Toward a progressive psychoanalysis.* Hove, East Sussex; New York: Routledge.

Beebe, B., & Lachmann, F. (2002). *Infant research and adult treatment: Co-constructing interactions.* Hillsdale, NJ: The Analytic Press.

Bernasconi, R. (2006). Strangers and Slaves in the Land of Egypt: Levinas and the Politics of Otherness. In A. Horowitz & G. Horowitz (Eds.), *Difficult justice:*

Commentaries on Levinas and politics (pp. 246–261). Toronto: University of Toronto Press.

Bernstein, R. J. (2002). *Radical evil: A philosophical interrogation.* Cambridge, UK; Malden, MA: Polity Press; Blackwell.

Bion, W. R. (1959). Attacks on Linking. *International Journal of Psychoanalysis, 40,* 308–315.

Bodnar, S. (2008). Wasted and Bombed: Clinical Enactments of Changing Relationship to the Earth. *Psychoanalytic Dialogues, 18,* 484–512.

Bollas, C. (1987). *The shadow of the object: Psychoanalysis of the unthought known.* London: Free Association Books.

Boris, H. N. (1994). *Envy.* Northvale, NJ: Aronson.

Boulanger, G. (2008). Witnesses to Reality: Working Psychodynamically with Survivors of Terror. *Psychoanalytic Dialogues, 18,* 638–657.

Brandchaft, B., Doctors, S., & Sorter, D. (2010). *Toward an emancipatory psychoanalysis: Brandchaft's intersubjective vision.* New York: Routledge.

Brenner, C. (1962). Freud's Concept of Repression and Defense, Its Theoretical and Observational Language. *Psychoanalytic Quarterly, 31,* 562–563.

Bromberg, P. (2006). *Awakening the dreamer: Clinical journeys.* Hillsdale, NJ: The Analytic Press.

Brothers, L. (2001). *Mistaken identity: The mind-brain problem reconsidered.* Albany, NY: State University of New York Press.

Broucek, F. (1991). *Shame and the self.* New York: Guilford Press.

Buechler, S. (2008). The Legacies of Shaming Psychoanalytic Candidates. *Contemporary Psychoanalysis, 44,* 56–64.

Butler, J. (2005). *Giving an account of oneself.* New York: Fordham University Press.

Catholic Church Pope (2013– : Francis). (2015). *Encyclical on climate change and inequality: On care for our common home.* Brooklyn, NY: Melville House Publishing.

Chefetz, R. A. (2000). Disorder in the Therapist's View of the Self. *Psychoanalytic Inquiry,* 20(2), 305–329.

Cilliers, P. (2007). *Thinking complexity.* Mansfield, MA: ISCE Publishing.

Coburn, W. J. (2014). *Psychoanalytic complexity: Clinical attitudes for therapeutic change.* New York: Routledge.

Cocks, G. (1997). *Psychotherapy in the Third Reich: The Göring Institute* (2nd ed.). New Brunswick: Transaction Publishers.

Corpt, E. (2013). Peasant in the Analyst's Chair: Reflections, Personal and Otherwise, on Class and the Formation of an Analytic Identity. *International Journal of Psychanalytic Self Psychology, 8,* 52–69.

Critchley, S. (2009). *The book of dead philosophers.* New York: Vintage Books.

Cushman, P. (2007). A Burning World, an Absent God: Midrash, Hermeneutics, and Relational Psychoanalysis. *Contemporary Psychoanalysis, 43,* 47–88.

Davis, D. B. (2006). *Inhuman bondage: The rise and fall of slavery in the New World.* New York: Oxford University Press.

DeYoung, P. A. (2015). *Understanding and treating chronic shame: A relational/neurobiological approach.* New York: Routledge, Taylor & Francis Group.

Dodds, J. (2011). *Psychoanalysis and ecology at the edge of chaos: Complexity theory, Deleuze/Guattari and psychoanalysis for a climate in crisis.* London; New York: Routledge.

Erikson, E. H. (1976). Psychoanalysis and Ethics—Avowed and Unavowed. *International Review of Psychoanalysis*, 3, 409–414.

Fairbairn, W. R. D. (1952). *Psychoanalytic studies of the personality.* London: Tavistock Publications.

Fogel, A. (1993). *Developing through relationships.* Chicago: University of Chicago Press.

Freud, S., & Riviere, J. (1922). *Introductory lectures on psycho-analysis: A course of twenty eight lectures delivered at the University of Vienna.* London: G. Allen & Unwin.

Fromm-Reichmann, F. (1950). *Principles of intensive psychotherapy.* Chicago: University of Chicago Press.

Fuller, R. W. (2003). *Somebodies and nobodies: Overcoming the abuse of rank.* Gabriola Island, Canada: New Society Publishers.

Fuller, R. W. (2006). *All rise: Somebodies, nobodies, and the politics of dignity* (1st ed.). San Francisco, CA: Berrett-Koehler.

Goldie, P. (2000). *The emotions: A philosophical exploration.* Oxford; New York: Clarendon Press.

Grand, S. (2008). Sacrificial Bodies: Terrorism, Counter-Terrorism, Torture. *Psychoanalytic Dialogues, 18*, 671–689.

Herman, J. (2009). Crime and Memory. In K. Golden & B. Bergo (Eds.), *The trauma controversy: Philosophical and interdisciplinary dialogues* (pp. 127–141). Albany: State University of New York Press.

Herman, J. (2011). Posttraumatic Stress Disorder as a Shame Disorder. In R. Dearing & J. Tangney (Eds.), *Shame in the therapy hour* (pp. 261–276). Washington, DC: American Psychological Association.

Howell, E. F., & Itzkowitz, S. (2016). *The dissociative mind in psychoanalysis: Understanding and working with trauma.* Abingdon, Oxon; New York: Routledge.

Jacobs, L. (2014). Learning to Love White Shame and Guilt: Skills for Working as a White Therapist in a Racially Divided Country. *International Journal of Psychoanalytic Self Psychology, 9*, 297–312.

Jacobson, E. (1957). Denial and Repression. *Journal of the American Psychoanalytic Association, 5*, 61–92.

Kahn, J., & Yardley, J. (2004, August 1). Amid China's Boom, No Helping Hand for Young Qingming. *The New York Times*, 1, 6.

Kilborne, B. (2008). The Evil Eye, Envy, and Shame: On Emotions and Explanation. In L. Wurmser & H. Jarass (Eds.), *Jealousy and envy: New views about two powerful feelings* (pp. 129–148). New York: The Analytic Press.

King, Martin Luther, Jr. (1986). A Time to Break Silence. In J. Washington (Ed.), *A testament of hope: The essential writings of Martin Luther King, Jr.* (pp. 231–244). San Francisco, CA: Harper Collins.

Klein, M. (1957). *Envy and gratitude, a study of unconscious sources.* New York: Basic Books.

Kohut, H. (1971). *The analysis of the self; a systematic approach to the psychoanalytic treatment of narcissistic personality disorders.* New York: International Universities Press.

Kohut, H. (1977). *The restoration of the self.* New York: International Universities Press.

Kohut, T. (2003). Psychoanalysis as Psychohistory or Why Psychotherapists Cannot Afford to Ignore Culture. *Annual Psychoanalysis, 31*, 225–236.

Kohut, T. A. (2012). *A German generation: An experiential history of the twentieth century.* New Haven, CT: Yale University Press.

Kuriloff, E. A. (2014). *Contemporary psychoanalysis and the legacy of the Third Reich: History, memory, tradition.* New York: Routledge, Taylor & Francis Group.

Lansky, M. (1999). Shame and the Idea of a Central Affect. *Psychoanalytic Inquiry, 19*, 347–361.

Lansky, M. R., & Morrison, A. P. (1997). *The widening scope of shame.* Hillsdale, NJ: Analytic Press.

Lertzman, R. (2015). *Environmental melancholia: Psychoanalytic dimensions of engagement.* New York: Routledge.

Levi, P. (1988). *The drowned and the saved.* New York: Summit Books.

Levinas, E. (1990). *Difficult freedom: Essays on Judaism.* Baltimore: Johns Hopkins University Press.

Lewis, H. B. (1974). *Shame and guilt in neurosis.* New York: International Universities Press.

Lewis, M. (1992). *Shame: The exposed self.* New York: Free Press.

Lichtenberg, J. (1994). Shame and the Self. *Psychoanalytic Quarterly, 63*, 124–129.

Lichtenberg, J., Lachmann, F., & Fosshage, J. (1992). *Self and motivational systems: Toward a theory of psychoanalytic technique.* Hillsdale, NJ: The Analytic Press.

Lichtenberg, J., Lachmann, F., & Fosshage, J. (1996). *The clinical exchange: Techniques derived from self and motivational systems.* Hillsdale, NJ: The Analytic Press.

Lichtenberg, J., Lachmann, F., & Fosshage, J. (2002). *The spirit of inquiry.* Hillsdale, NJ: The Analytic Press.

Loewald, H. W. (1955). Hypnoid State, Repression, Abreaction and Recollection. *Journal of the American Psychoanalytic Association, 3*, 201–210.

Loewald, H. W. (1960). On the Therapeutic Action of Psycho-Analysis. *International Journal of Psychoanalysis, 41*, 16–33.

Loewald, H. W. (1970). Psychoanalytic Theory and the Psychoanalytic Process. *The Psychoanalytic Study of the Child, 25*, 45–68.

Loewald, H. W. (1972). The Experience of Time. *The Psychoanalytic Study of the Child, 27*, 401–410.

Loewald, H. W. (1979). Reflections on the Psychoanalytic Process and Its Therapeutic Potential. *The Psychoanalytic Study of the Child, 34*, 155–167.

Lovett, Ian. (2015, September 7). *A Los Angeles Plan to Reshape the Streetscape Sets off Fears of Gridlock.* Retrieved from http://www.nytimes.com/2015/09/08/us/a-los-angeles-plan-to-reshape-the-streetscape-sets-off-fears-of-gridlock.html?_r=0

Marks-Tarlow, T. (2012). Review of Joseph Dodds' "Psychoanalysis and Ecology at the Edge of Chaos." *International Journal of Psychanalytic Self Psychology, 7*, 565–572.

Marshall, G. (2014). *Don't even think about it: Why our brains are wired to ignore climate change* (1st U.S. ed.). New York: Bloomsbury USA.

Morrison, A. (1984). Working with Shame in Psychoanalytic Treatment. *Journal of the American Psychoanalytic Association, 32*, 479–505.

Morrison, A. (1989). *Shame: The underside of narcissism.* Hillsdale, NJ: The Analytic Press.

Morrison, A. (1994). The Breadth and Boundaries of a Self-Psychological Immersion in Shame: A One-and-a-Half-Person Perspective. *Psychoanalytic Dialogues, 4*, 19–35.

Morrison, A., & Lansky, M. (2008). Shame and Envy. In L. Wurmser & H. Jarass (Eds.), *Jealousy and envy: New views about two powerful feelings* (pp. 179–188). New York: Analytic Press.

Morrison, A. P. (1996). *The culture of shame* (1st ed.). New York: Ballantine Books.

Nussbaum, M. C. (2004). *Hiding from humanity: Disgust, shame, and the law.* Princeton, NJ: Princeton University Press.

Orange, D. M. (1995). *Emotional understanding: Studies in psychoanalytic epistemology.* New York: Guilford Press.

Orange, D. (2008). Whose Shame Is It Anyway? Lifeworlds of Humiliation and Systems of Restoration. *Contemporary Psychoanalysis, 44*, 83–100.

Orange, D. (2010). *"The Attitude of Heroes": Bernard Brandchaft and the Hermeneutics of Trust.* Paper presented at the International Conference on the Psychology of the Self, Antalya, Turkey.

Orange, D. (2013). Unsuspected Shame: Responding to Corpt's "Peasant in the Analyst's Chair: Reflections, Personal and Otherwise, on Class and the Formation of an Analytic Identity." *International Journal of Psychanalytic Self Psychology, 8*, 70–76.

Orange, D. (2016). *Nourishing the inner life of clinicians and humanitarians: The ethical turn in psychoanalysis.* London; New York: Routledge.

Orange, D. M., Atwood, G. E., & Stolorow, R. D. (1997). *Working intersubjectively: Contextualism in psychoanalytic practice.* Hillsdale, NJ: Analytic Press.

Ratzel, F. (1966). *Der Lebensraum. Eine biogeographische Studie.* Darmstadt: Wissenschaftliche Buchgesellschaft.

Sander, L. (1982). Polarity, Paradox, and the Organizing Process in Development. In J. Call, E. Galenson, & R. Tyson (Eds.), *Proceedings of the First World Congress on Infant Psychiatry* (pp. 871–908). New York: Basic Books.

Segal, H. (1987a). Silence Is the Real Crime. *International Review of Psychoanalysis, 14*, 3–12.

Segal, H. (1987b). Against the State of Nuclear Terror, by Joel Kovel, Free Association Books, 1987, 240 pages, pb £3.95. *Free Associations, 1*, 137–142.

Schoeck, H. (1987). *Envy: A theory of social behaviour.* Indianapolis: Liberty Fund.

Searles, H. (1972). Unconscious Processes in Relation to the Environmental Crisis. *Psychoanalytic Review, 59*, 361–374.

Searles, H. F. (1960). *The nonhuman environment, in normal development and in schizophrenia*. New York: International Universities Press.

Soldz, S. (2008). Healers or Interrogators: Psychology and the United States Torture Regime. *Psychoanalytic Dialogues, 18*, 592–613.

Spinoza, B. D., & Parkinson, G. H. R. (2000). *Ethics*. Oxford; New York: Oxford University Press.

Staemmler, F.-M. (2012). *Empathy in psychotherapy: How therapists and clients understand each other*. New York: Springer.

Steiner, J. (1993). *Psychic retreats: Pathological organizations in psychotic, neurotic, and borderline patients*. London; New York: Routledge.

Stolorow, R., & Atwood, G. (1992). *Contexts of being: The intersubjective foundations of psychological life*. Hillsdale, NJ: The Analytic Press.

Stolorow, R., Atwood, G., & Orange, D. (2002). *Worlds of experience: Interweaving philosophical and clinical dimensions in psychoanalysis*. New York: Basic Books.

Summers, F. (2008). Making Sense of the APA: A History of the Relationship Between Psychology and the Military. *Psychoanalytic Dialogues, 18*, 614–637.

Tomkins, S. (1962–3). *Affect, imagery, consciousness* (Vol. 1 and 2). New York: Springer.

Visick, V. (2015). Some Reflections on *Laudoto Si'*. In J. Cobb & I. Castuera (Eds.), *For our common home: Process-relational responses to Laudato Si'* (pp. 411–415). Anoka, MN: Process Century Press.

Volkan, V. D. (1994). Repression and Dissociation: Implications for Personality Theory, Psychopathology, and Health. *Journal of the American Psychoanalytic Association, 42*, 301–304.

Weintrobe, S. (2012). *Engaging with climate change: Psychoanalytic and interdisciplinary perspectives*. Abingdon, Oxon; New York: Routledge.

Wille, R. (2014). The Shame of Existing: An Extreme Form of Shame. *International Journal of Psychoanalysis, 95*, 695–717.

Williams, B. (1993). *Shame and necessity*. Berkeley: University of California Press.

Woodruff, P. (2014). *Reverence: Renewing a forgotten virtue* (2nd ed.). New Nork, NY: Oxford University Press.

Wurmser, L. (1991). Shame. The Underside of Narcissism. *Psychoanalytic Quarterly, 60*, 667–672.

Wurmser, L., & Jarass, H. (2008). *Jealousy and envy: New views about two powerful emotions*. New York: Lawrence Erlbaum Associates.

Chapter 4

Radical ethics for our climate emergency

With a few small guilty reservations, most people consider themselves ethical. They would say that morality, fairness, and being good remain important to them even as they pursue whatever they pursue, in daily life and in large political problems like climate justice. Asking oneself more questions, however, especially if one probes beyond ideals absorbed from family, religion, or popular culture, if one asks what makes some course of action better or worse, the answers divide into the major philosophical schools of ethics: duty ethics, utilitarianism, and virtue ethics. We might call these systems "the ethics of everyday life."

In the modern era, Immanuel Kant spoke for what philosophers call deontological, or duty, ethics. His "categorical imperative" requires me to act as if I intended everyone to act similarly in like circumstances. As a basic requirement, no one gets a free pass. I cannot expect of others what I do not require of myself. "Act only according to that maxim whereby you can, at the same time, will that it should become a universal law" (Kant, Ellington, & Kant, 1983, p. 421). This imperative, categorical because it describes an absolute, imperative duty, also reflects a kind of negative Golden Rule: do not do unto others what you would not have them do unto you. In another formulation, Kant demanded that all humans be treated as ends in themselves, never as means only, contributing significantly to the sensibilities encoded in the United Nations Declaration on Human Rights under the leadership of Eleanor Roosevelt after World War II. As Bernasconi (2010) notes, Kant, seeing that our living on a globe had moral implications: that its surface had to be held in common, for the good of all, argued that Europeans usurping the places where indigenous peoples had lived was clearly unjust. Unfortunately, however, those enlightened "cosmopolitans" who would manage everything justly, in his view, belonged undoubtedly to the light-skinned peoples.

Important 20th-century ethical systems, especially those of John Rawls and Jürgen Habermas, owe much of their inspiration to Kant. Rawls (Rawls, 1971; Rawls & Kelly, 2001), fusing Kantian ethics with the individualistic, social contract political ethics discussed in Chapter 1, imagined an original situation. Under the "veil of ignorance" about our personal condition (racial, sexual, economic, etc.), we would agree on the arrangements for a just and fair society. Any inequalities that emerge would be adjusted for the sake of the least advantaged. Habermas (Habermas, 1984, 1987), ever haunted by the history of Germany in his lifetime (1929–), likewise claims that a just society includes all its voices in communicative action. As long as I can remember, he has functioned as Europe's public philosopher, calling out every form of return to authoritarian ways and to German hegemony, right down to Germany's behavior in the Greek debt crisis.

In one of the first philosophical considerations of environmental degradation, Hans Jonas, refugee from Nazi Germany, reformulated Kant's maxim to read: "Act so that the effects of your action are compatible with the permanence of genuine human life" or "Act so that the effects of your action are not destructive of the future possibility of such life" (Jonas, 1984, p. 11). Again, like all duty ethics, this maxim addresses universal responsibility.

Clearly, duty/deontological ethics offers much to climate justice thinkers, prohibiting the use of the earth in ways that radically profit some people (Europeans and North Americans) at the expense of others. Critics, however, have always noticed the tendency toward rigidity in this ethic, along with its isolation of persons and acts from their contexts and from complexity. May I lie to protect a neighbor from violence, or a child from unnecessary humiliation?

A new relation to our earth that treasures all its people will require recontextualizing everything—energy resources, agriculture, and consumption, for example—all with a connectedness and complexity mentality.

Next we encounter the utilitarians (Bentham, 1876; Mill, 2007), according to whom we measure the ethical by risks and benefits, classically put: the greatest good for the greatest number. The early utilitarians particularly concerned themselves with the plight of industrial workers, and the subjection of women (Mill, 1970). Today their heirs, the consequentialists, dominate discussions in business and medical ethics, while Peter Singer (Singer, 1975, 2004), perhaps the best-known living consequentialist and deeply concerned about the destructive consequences of globalization, argues for the ethical treatment of animals. Utilitarian/consequentialist thinking can cut both ways in the environmental crisis: it may extend the kinds of consequences we are willing to consider, especially worrying about the extinction of so many species, but it may too easily dismiss some people and species as dispensable, and damage to them as inevitable, in the service of important goods. It also risks ignoring unconscious privilege, overweighting some goods as the expense of those important to those whose voices tend to be unheard. It then runs afoul of the Kantian intuition, shared by the world's religious and spiritual traditions, seeing each human being, as well as our "common home" (Catholic Church Pope [2013– : Francis], 2015) as precious and irreplaceable.[1]

Western philosophy further offers virtue ethics, indebted to Aristotle. This view shifts the questions away from ethical decision-making. When, if ever, may we break a promise? How do we decide the lesser of two evils, or whether goods outweigh evils in a particular instance? Instead Aristotelian ethics asks: What characterizes a good human being? What kind of life is a good life for human beings to want? What kind of person can we call good? How does such a person act wisely? Obviously these latter questions bear closely on the problems we face in this time of climate crisis. A virtue ethicist might argue, for example, that the virtues of justice and

peacefulness require us to moderate our desires for more of everything when others lack the means of subsistence. Virtue ethics can
surely help to rule out hubristic solutions like bioengineering that
would shield the Global North from carbon damage, or moving to
Mars, while also challenging evasion. But virtue ethics, while indispensable, may not suffice to move enough of us to take the radical
actions needed right now. Its laudable preference for moderation
may impede our perception of, and needed response to, our current
emergency. Given virtue ethics' foundation on the presumption of
freedom—it arose in a slaveholding society—it may not be able to
see its own situated presumptions. It needs challenging dialogue, just
as the others do, if they are not to further damage the poor.

Clearly we need additional ethical ideas, if we are not simply to
confront the religious sensibility Pope Francis brings—still deny-
ing the full equality of women and their control of their bodies,
unfortunately—with the entitled fundamentalism that dominates
political discourse in the United States, resisting every suggestion
that we require repentance, conversion, and a radical turn to simple,
humble, communal, and earth-sensitive forms of life. A simple appeal
to religious pluralism—your preacher next to my pope, or vice
versa—leaves us at an impasse. Still, we have additional resources
from Western philosophy and from Asian religions, resonant enough
to engage both secular (world-oriented) and religious people: dialogue, the do-no-harm ethics, and radical responsibility.

Deep ecology

Many serious interdisciplinary thinkers (Barnhill, Gottlieb, & American Academy of Religion. National Meeting, 2001; Devall & Sessions, 1985; Macy & Johnstone, 2012; Naess, Drengson, & Devall,
2008) have embraced "deep ecology" as an ethics for the climate
crisis. According to this perspective, the earth and all its creatures
have equally inherent value, non-instrumental and deserving of reverent treatment. We can hear resonances of the earth relatedness of
many indigenous peoples, of Buddhists, of St. Francis of Assisi, and

of Protestant talk of care and stewardship of creation, as opposed to domination and exploitation. Its eight-point platform (Naess & Sessions, 1993) runs as follows:

1. The well-being and flourishing of human and nonhuman life on Earth have value in themselves (synonyms: inherent worth, intrinsic value, inherent value). These values are independent of the usefulness of the nonhuman world for human purposes.
2. Richness and diversity of life-forms contribute to the realization of these values and are also values in themselves.
3. Humans have no right to reduce this richness and diversity except to satisfy vital needs.
4. Present human interference with the nonhuman world is excessive, and the situation is rapidly worsening.
5. The flourishing of human life and cultures is compatible with a substantial decrease of the human population. The flourishing of nonhuman life requires such a decrease.
6. Policies must therefore be changed. The changes in policies affect basic economic, technological, and ideological structures. The resulting state of affairs will be deeply different from the present.
7. The ideological change is mainly that of appreciating life quality (dwelling in situations of inherent worth) rather than adhering to an increasingly higher standard of living. There will be a profound awareness of the difference between big and great.
8. Those who subscribe to the foregoing points have an obligation directly or indirectly to participate in the attempt to implement the necessary changes.

Influential as this perspective continues to be, challenging anthropocentric presumptions responsible for the climate crisis and uniting extraordinary leaders in challenging the destructive status quo, it has been forcefully challenged on various grounds. First, even for those, like Pope Francis, who hold strong affection for the earth and all our brother and sister species, this approach decentralizes the problem of social justice. By making all species, plants and animals and humans, exactly equivalent in value, we can then instrumentalize other human beings in the service of population reduction or other goals.[2] Deep ecology seems simple, clear, and spiritual, but it may be too simple. Complexity theorists, with their own ethical discourse (Halloy & Lockwood, 2007), challenge us to realize that social Darwinism,[3] engendering both the climate crisis and the extremes of economic inequality and resultant suffering, can seem "natural." Dangerous philosophical assumptions may be embedded in a point of view that claims to know what is "natural"—remember the authoritarian and masculinist presumptions in Roman Catholic natural law theory. Even worse, equating the natural with the good, without having questioned either term's meaning, could take us out of the frying pan into the fire.

Second, the deep ecology point of view understates both the reality of connectedness and the need for solidarity. Its fundamental principle of equal worth may set up, or rather reinforce, a competition between humans and our natural home, shared with other species. If the same intrinsic value belongs to all species, we are not allowed to prioritize the survival of our impoverished human brothers and sisters. Knowing some proponents of this view, I understand clearly that they could not intend this. We need, instead, to balance care and reverence for our human others with care for our air, water, plants, and animals, so that we can all survive and thrive together. Surely this is what they mean too.

Third, critics like Murray Bookchin (Bookchin, 2007) object that deep ecology underestimates the role of authoritarianism, greed, and all forms of dominating hierarchy in our crisis. These problems result from mistreatment of humans by humans, treating the natural world as collateral damage. Or perhaps vice versa. Instead of deep ecology, far too spiritual for him, he propounds a practical solution-focused, social ecology.

Admitting that none of the approaches available so far have moved us toward the massive change we urgently need, let us consider three more resources.

Dialogue: listening for the voice of the other

For a quarter century, relationalist Donnel B. Stern (Stern, 1990, 1991, 1997, 2005), contextualists Philip Cushman (Cushman, 1996, 2005, 2007), and I (D. Orange, 2009; D. M. Orange, 1995, 2010) have offered Hans-Georg Gadamer's philosophical hermeneutics as a dialogical phenomenology for clinical work. Cushman and I have argued that its moral sensibility makes it distinctly preferable to postmodernist deconstructionisms, from which any vision of the good human life or any grounds for criticism tend to go missing. Everything is ultimately undecidable. In this age of the "ethical turn" in psychoanalysis and in the humanistic psychotherapies, a period that draws a fast-growing crowd of clinicians and scholars to think together about "Psychology and the Other" in Boston every two years, perhaps we rather need the ethical grounding offered by Gadamerian hermeneutics. Can hermeneutic ethics offer what we need for climate crisis?

This hermeneutics, indebted to long traditions in religions, literature, and jurisprudence, seeks understanding in dialogue. Profoundly anti-authoritarian and suspicious of every form of idolatry (Cushman, 2007), hermeneutics still retains reverence (Woodruff, 2014) for the traditions that each voice in the dialogue brings to the table. "The possibility that the other person may be right is the soul of hermeneutics," Gadamer said frequently (July 9, 1989, Heidelberg Conference, quoted in Grondin, 1994, p. 124). At the same time, it plays with the texts, stories, and preconceived ideas, holding these lightly so that new configurations may emerge and appear. It treats the voice of the other, even when that voice opposes mine, as the site of learning and the source of possible truth. Utterly contrasted with the hegemonies of power or money, hermeneutics teaches us receptive attitudes toward difference, trust in our common humanity, open ears to learn from the other. Gadamer wrote:

> We say that we "conduct" a conversation, but the more genuine a conversation is, the less its conduct lies within the will of either

partner. Thus a genuine conversation is never the one that we wanted to conduct. Rather, it is generally more correct to say that we fall into conversation, or even that we become involved in it. The way one word follows another, with the conversation taking its own twists and reaching its own conclusion, may well be conducted in some way, but the partners conversing are far less the leaders of it than the led. No one knows in advance what will "come out" of a conversation. Understanding or its failure is like an event that happens to us.[4]

(TM 383)

How can dialogic hermeneutics help us in this moment of urgent environmental change and emergency? We must first note that, although Gadamer's great work, *Truth and Method*, set out to contest the dominion of the methodical and reductionistic thinking of the hard sciences, and to claim that the larger and deeper truth belonged to art, poetry, and to all that welcomes interpretation, his project was always full of ethics. Having lived through and seen firsthand in Germany—his life spanned 1900–2002—as great an ethical travesty as anyone could remember, he turned to the Greeks to renew the primacy of ethics, and the account of living well as *phronesis*, or practical wisdom. Dialogue he took from his beloved Plato, phronesis from Aristotle. For both, any kind of knowing worth having was ethical knowing.

But our misuse of the earth has broken this link between wise practical engineering and the ethical. We have learned to measure and to calculate without considering goodness, without asking how our extraction of shale gas, our reinjection into the earth of toxic water from oil drilling, may cause endless earthquakes, how tar sands oil desecrates lands that belong to indigenous peoples, and with them to all of us. Where is the dialogue and reverence in coal mining practices that leave whole communities ill, mountains gone, and rivers poisoned? Gadamer again: "The task of bringing people to a self-understanding of themselves may help us to gain our freedom in relation to everything that has taken us in unquestioningly"

(Gadamer, 1982, pp. 149–150). Gadamer's later work, as Ingrid Scheibler (2000) also notes, often expressed concern about increasing environmental destruction, and connected this problem to social justice, writing: "The food problem of mankind, for example, can only be overcome by giving up the lavish wastefulness that has covered the earth" (Gadamer & Palmer, 2007, p. 88).[5]

But questioning ourselves may be resurgent. Hermeneuts note that finding just and reasonable solutions to environmental problems involving many competing interests and needs—California's farmers versus its fishing industry, for example, or New Zealand's farms versus its tourist industry and the claims of its indigenous Maori (www. academic conferences.org/ecrm/ecrm2006/Arunachalam.pdf)—call for open and respectful dialogue if workable solutions are to emerge.

And yet, though solutions must remain dialogic if they are not to generate more injustice or stalemate, dialogue may not be enough.

Asian philosophies: *ahimsa* and non-possessiveness

For the West to find its way out of the narcissistic consumption-oriented way of life, unable to envision "small is beautiful" (Schumacher, 1973) and "do the least possible harm to living things" (*ahimsa*), we may need to turn to the resources of Asian religions and philosophies, radically challenging our prevailing ways of life. One among several such possibilities, Jainism, perhaps the oldest of the earth's continuous religious traditions, teaches three fundamental principles: (1) avoidance of violence to all living beings, so far as possible; (2) non-possessiveness; and (3) constant recognition that one's perception is only a perspective (the blind men and the elephant). The Jain study of violence—physical, verbal, and mental or spiritual—leads to extensive meditation on one's own temptations to violence. It also heavily influenced the particular form Mahatma Ghandi's non-violent leadership took.

Less concerned with actual possessions than with attitudes, non-possessiveness concerns our desire to have or be more, greater, and especially more than someone else, the problem we discussed as envy in our previous chapter. Much of Jain spiritual practice devotes itself to liberation from such desires. This second principle seriously challenges consumerist mentalities and identification of self-worth with one's "net worth." The third principle, the many facets of truth, in my vocabulary "perspectivalism," fits well with the dialogic mentality we need to find just, non-dominating solutions to the problems of climate change.

Violence and possessiveness increase each soul's karmic burden, until through asceticism, it liberates itself from the necessity of reincarnation. Though Jains, evidently the originators of the concept of karmic causality in other Asian religions, conceive karma as an individual matter, it takes a very small leap to understand our current environmental destruction as the karmic consequence of violence and possessiveness on a large scale. From our Asian sisters and brothers we may learn both individual and communal liberation as they teach us an examination of conscience at least as rigorous as any practiced in Christianity.

Radical ethics and politics[6]

Inverting all standard ethical accounts, radical (indebted to philosopher/ Talmudist Emmanuel Levinas [1906–1995]) ethics, "first philosophy," upends moral reasoning by starting from the suffering Other invading my self-satisfied life (Smith, 2011), not from the putative moral agent. Emptied of ego by a pre-originary responsibility, I am commanded by the other's starvation. William Edelglass (Edelglass, 2012) provides a compact argument for what I am calling a radical ethics of climate change:

> Because Levinasian ethics begins in, and ever returns to, the suffering other, the suffering of those whose lives are negatively impacted by climate change rupture arguments that justify, or justify neglecting, individual GHG [greenhouse gas] emissions.

Levinas acknowledges that in nourishing ourselves we take food that can feed others.

(p. 210)

In other words, my irrecusable responsibility[7] to the vulnerable and suffering other does not go away just because I need to drive or fly somewhere. Nor is it lessened because this vulnerable other ekes out a bare existence in the Southern Hemisphere, less visible to me. Philosopher Robert Bernasconi (2010) writes:

> A hungry child in a distant land is no longer out of our reach. If globalization means living in a world in which the terms far and near, stranger and neighbor, no longer have the same meaning for us as they once did because everyone is now recognized as within the same circle, then the hunger of the most marginalized members of the global society must become its fundamental reference point.
>
> (p. 77)

The other's precarious life (Butler, 2004) questions me, accuses me, persecutes me. A close consequence of this endless responsibility links it to the political.

"There is no place," writes Bernasconi, "for an ethical discourse that is not also inextricably linked with a recognition of the political context that it is its task to interrupt" (Bernasconi, 2006, p. 256). Despite misunderstandings of Levinasian ethics as individualistic, concerning only the single neighbor or stranger, Bernasconi explains that experiences of persecution instead link us to others enslaved, impoverished, homeless, in solidarity. Watching the thousands of families seeking shelter in Europe in 2015, those who remember their own suffering may be better able to respond. Instead, oblivious to the causes of the misery that brings children and adults to our southern border here in the United States, we compete to boast about who can build the largest and most robust wall against them. Most of us, unless affected by tornadoes, hurricanes, and wildfires, have no memory of this kind of suffering. When the sufferers look much like us—perhaps white and even affluent, we rush to help them rebuild. But many of those devastated by hurricanes like Katrina are already poor and/or dark-skinned, so we treat them just as we treat the refugees. How do we come to see them as our brothers and sisters? Can memory, either of our own sufferings or of past courage and generosity, begin to activate us in the nick of time? In Merold Westphal's words, "Conscience need not make cowards of us all; it can make us brothers and sisters" (Westphal, 2008, p. 133).

This radical ethics of response to the other implies disrupting massive political injustice[8] when we are able to see it. It means that others' suffering persecutes me, takes me hostage, requires substitution, one-for-the-other. It demands hospitality to people displaced by war, poverty, terror. Even if we cannot speak their languages, we can see their desperate faces. We must remember. In our own history, we can remember quiet activists sitting at segregated lunch counters, sitting at the front of segregated buses, disrupting injustice. Now we find indigenous peoples of Canada, the United States, and elsewhere, sitting down to close the roads to tar-sands drilling equipment. But we need more than "only the persecuted" (Levinas, 1981, p. 111; extended and elaborated by Bernasconi, 1995), to stand in solidarity against injustice. How do we find our ethical bones? Even when the photo of the drowned three-year-old refugee on a Mediterranean beach stops us for a moment in our tracks, how do we keep our ethical imagination awake, determined that a world in which some lives are regarded as expendable cannot continue? We need an ethic that arises from these extreme situations, because we face one now. Let us hear these words:

> justice remains justice only, in a society where there is no distinction between those close and those far off, but in which there also remains the impossibility of passing by the closest.

The equality of all is borne by my inequality, the surplus of my duties over my rights. The forgetting of self moves justice.

(Levinas, 1981, p. 159)

This ethic, counter to the egoism we explored in our opening chapter, means a radical dispossession, a hitherto unthinkable hospitality, with the tent flaps open on all sides as the Talmudists told the story of Abraham and the three angels. Levinas, a Lithuanian Jew, philosopher, and teacher of Talmud, never forgot that French nuns had hidden his wife and daughter while he spent five years in a Nazi labor camp and his family was murdered in Lithuania.[9] He knew what hospitality could be worth. Still, to describe his meaning, he returned in his Talmudic lectures to Abraham, the ancestor, not only of those belonging to the three monotheistic faiths, but of every fully human person. He wrote:

Father of believers? Certainly. But above all the one who knew how to receive and feed men: the one whose tent was wide open on all sides. Through these openings he looked out for passersby in order to receive them. The meal offered by Abraham? We know especially of one meal, the one he offered to the three angels—without suspecting their condition as angels. . . . Abraham must have taken the three passersby for three Bedouins, for three nomads from the Negev Desert—three Arabs, in other words! He runs toward them. He calls them "your Lordships." The heirs of Abraham—men to whom their ancestor bequeathed a difficult tradition of duties toward the other man, which one is never done with, an order in which one is never free. In this order above all else, duty takes the form of obligation toward the body, the obligation of feeding and sheltering. So defined, the heirs of Abraham are of all nations:[10] any man truly man is no doubt of the line of Abraham.

(Levinas, 1990, p. 99)

Here Levinas refers, in a Talmudic and biblical context, to his philosophical and ethical claim that the other has an infinite claim on my
protection and care, that, as he often said, there exists a "curvature
of intersubjective space" (Levinas, 1969), a radical asymmetry, in
which the stranger's destitution, the other's homelessness, transcends
my need for comfort absolutely. "Abraham was the one whose tent
remained open day and night, the one who fed his guests without
asking who they were beforehand" (Chalier, 2002, p. 107).

We are already reminded of the millions of refugees from today's
war-torn and desertifying Middle East. So we go on to confront
the difficulty in which the question about Abraham had arisen: the
rabbi's son has hired some workers, and agreed to feed them. The
rabbi says:

> My son, even if you prepared a meal for them equal to the one
> King Solomon served, you would not have fulfilled your obli-
> gation toward them, for they are the descendants of Abraham,
> Isaac, and Jacob. As long as they have not begun the work, go
> and specify: you are only entitled to bread and dry vegetables.[11]
>
> (Talmud Tractate *Baba Metsia*, pp. 83a–83b,
> Mishna, quoted in Levinas, 1990, p. 94)

Levinas commented that the rabbi is so frightened because he
understands that his son has committed himself to infinite hospitality,[12] to an infinite ethical obligation that will be well understood by these descendants of Abraham, Isaac, and Jacob, who
know about the tent open on all sides. Levinas went on to recall
the words of a famous Lithuanian rabbi, Israel Salanter: "The material needs of my neighbor are my spiritual needs" (Levinas, 1990,
p. 99). So the father counsels his son immediately to set limits
and conditions on his obligation. "What is truly human," Levinas
continued, "is beyond human strength" (p. 100). But the subject
of limits already arises in the Talmudic context, to be resumed
in Derrida's commentary on Levinas below. But confronting the
limits of the ethical means asking what we *can* do; it does not mean

throwing up our hands and locking down the tent, refusing to be descendants of Abraham.

In his philosophical work, Levinas, who lived and worked in France until he died in 1995, propounded one big philosophical idea, namely, that before everything comes "a radically asymmetrical relation of infinite responsibility to the other person" (Critchley & Bernasconi, 2002). In his great work, *Totality and Infinity*, he contrasted what he called "totalizing"—treating others as something to be studied, categorized, or comprehended—with responding to the suffering "visage" of the other.

This "other," no alter-ego that resembles me, no unrelated ego entering social contracts in freedom, bursts the bounds of the phenomenology Levinas had learned from Edmund Husserl and from Heidegger. This irreducible "face" always transcends our concepts, representations, categories, and ideas. The human other presents me with an infinite demand for protection and care, just as the Talmudic rabbi understood his son's responsibility. Each face says: you shall not kill. You shall not allow me to die alone. The three-year-old on the beach, the children and parents on our southern border, these face me as my sisters and brothers.

> The neighbor concerns me before all assumption, all commitment consented to or refused. . . . It is not because the neighbor would be recognized as belonging to the same genus as me that he concerns me. He is precisely other. The community with him begins in my obligation to him. The neighbor is a brother.
>
> (Levinas, 1981, p. 87)

Every reduction—by systematizing, classifying, pointing, even describing—is, for Levinas, violence, a violation, a form of murder. (We easily understand the outraged response even today to refugee quotas, and to rigid distinctions between migrants and refugees. These can evoke selections.) The neighbor, instead, exposes me "to the summons of this responsibility as though placed under a blazing sun that eradicates every residue of mystery, every ulterior motive, every loosening of the thread that would allow evasion" (Levinas, 1996, p. 104). The response must be "Me voici" (me here), "how can I help you?" "welcome": I am indeed my brother's keeper, and there is no escape. No escape from climate crisis, no escape from the suffering and injustice our comfortable and mindless "lifestyles" are creating.

As mentioned above, the relation to the other (*Autrui*) creates what Levinas called a "curvature of intersubjective space" (Levinas & Nemo, 1985, p. 291). What can this mean? An essay called "Transcendence and Height" explains that the other always ranks higher than me when in need: "The Other (*l'Autre*) thus presents itself as human Other (*Autrui*); it shows a face and opens a dimension of *height*, that is to is to say, it *infinitely* overflows the bounds of knowledge" (Levinas, Peperzak, Critchley, & Bernasconi, 1996, p. 12, emphasis in original). The ethical relation is not between equals, but is radically asymmetrical, that is, from "inside that relation, as it takes place, at this very moment, you place an obligation on me that makes you more than me, more than my equal" (Critchley, 2002, p. 14). Although we need law and justice and equal treatment ethics— as a kind of support system for the unlimited ethical relation—the fundamental ethical relation of proximity to the devastated and dislocated neighbor is so radically tilted and irreversible as not to seem equal in any phenomenologically describable way.

My response to the face is simply "me voici" (*hineni*), not "Here I am" as it is usually translated, but rather, as Paul Ricoeur pointed out, "it's me here" (Ricoeur, 1992). It welcomes radically. The face of the other calls me, demands from me, takes me hostage, persecutes me. Response is my refusal to be unmoved, or indifferent, to the face of the other, to the other's "useless suffering" (Levinas, 1988). What I am or need, or how I feel toward the other, is not in question.[13] Now we can see why speaking abstractly of the climate crisis will not be enough: only the other's misery will be enough to command us: "The Other is the poor and destitute one, and nothing which concerns this Stranger can leave the I indifferent" (Levinas et al., 1996, p. 17).

Central concepts of this perspective admittedly can sound extreme, for example, substitution. Sometimes radical ethics seems to require that I be prepared to give my last ounce of bread so that the other may have a chance to survive, or to volunteer to face the firing squad in your place. (In fact, the longer I read Levinas, the more I think he would say this is not a misinterpretation—I should always be ready, as Nelson Mandela was ready to stay in prison before accepting compromises that would keep his people subjugated, or Dietrich Bonhoeffer was prepared to remain in prison indefinitely, to face torture or death, rather than to say anything that would betray his fellow conspirators in the plot to assassinate Hitler.) Working with severely traumatized patients, I sometimes noticed that a background working attitude of empathic resonance or attunement, often playful in a Winnicottian sense, seemed to break down. I found myself impelled to wish, and sometimes even to say, that I wished that I could take at least some of their torment onto myself, make it lessen at least for a while, to let them be less alone. What is this? Had I become a terminal masochist? Had I become a grandiose messianic figure in my own imagination? Should I quickly seek out another psychoanalysis? Or is there also something to understand here about the nature of our work, about clinical hospitality, something that makes it continuous with the political and personal hospitality of the extreme situation? Is there also something about the other's hunger, closely related to my life of luxury, to my mindless consumption, that demands an ethics of substitution, of allowing myself to feel persecuted by the other's suffering?

Let us listen to the formulation in his essay entitled "Substitution" (Levinas et al., 1996): "It is through the condition of being a hostage that there can be pity, compassion, pardon, and proximity in the world—even the little there is, even the simple 'after you sir'" (p. 91). Responsibility for the other, said Levinas, "is the essential structure of subjectivity" (Levinas & Nemo, 1985, p. 95). In other words, according to Bernasconi, he was not preaching sacrifice, but did want to account for the possibility of unexpected goodness. If we were as essentially for-ourselves as Sartre (2001) and others have believed, Levinasian ethics would not be possible. Neither heroic behavior—like that of those who had risked their lives to save

Levinas's wife and daughter, nor everyday "après vous, monsieur" hospitality and courtesy—would be possible. We would live in the Hobbsean world of all against all, or at least in the familiar "What's in it for me and my family?" world that so often dominates politics in those nations who benefit most from industrialization and carbon polluting.

Subjectivity transforms in this radical ethic. Only in the suffering of the other, and in my response, do I (a moi, not an ego) come into being, "me voici," called into being by the other's naked and vulnerable face. The sovereign self, with its "place in the sun," always trying to have more, would be indifferent to the plight of the other. What minimal subjectivity remains to me, instead, comes about via my response to the widow, the orphan, and the stranger. Ricoeur, in his encounter with Levinas, speaks of the "modesty of self constancy" (1992, p. 168), asking "Who am I, so inconstant, that notwithstanding you count on me?" (p. 168). I am reminded of Georges Bernanos, whose country priest without faith of his own speaks to the dying congregant: " 'Be at peace,' I told her. And she had knelt to receive this peace. May she keep it forever. It will be I that give it her. Oh, miracle—thus to be able to give what we ourselves do not possess, sweet miracle of our empty hands! Hope which was shriveling in my heart flowered again in hers" (Bernanos & Morris, 1937, p. 180). Again, in the instance of a gift, "the other can be said to dispossess me on occasion so that giving is not an act, but an ethical event whereby I lose my sense of mine in the face of the other" (Critchley & Bernasconi, 2002, p. 240). Something happens to me in the face of the other's need so that my giving has the quality of participating (though this would not be Levinas's own formulation). My background role becomes habitual. Derrida later paraphrased Levinas: "the relation to the other is deference" (Derrida, 1999, p. 46). Judith Butler writes of dispossession; Levinas perhaps provided the inspiration: " relationship with the other puts me into question, empties me of myself and empties me without end, showing me ever new resources. I did not know I was so rich, but I no longer have the right to keep anything for myself" (Levinas, 1987, 94).

But the question of endless responsibility to and for the other troubles us clinicians, as we can see from the Talmudic lectures that it troubled Levinas too. Catherine Chalier writes:

> In his Talmudic reading, Levinas insists on the importance that Guemara [one component of the Talmud, also called Gemorra] grants to the contract which precedes the hiring of the worker and which, linked to the custom of the place, specifies the salary owed to him, the food that will be given to him, etc. In other words, the descendant of Abraham knows that there is no limit to his obligations towards the worker. The contract thus comes to limit my obligations toward the worker and not, as one might assume, to institute a minimum of obligation toward him. [This is a fine distinction!]. This means, very precisely, that obligations towards the other are infinite and do not depend on good will or choice. They precede freedom and consecrate the descendant of Abraham [every good human being] to an infinite service, to a responsibility that is greater than the commitments that have actively been taken on. . . . contracts and customs attempt in fact to introduce some limit to this initial or more exactly, immemorial, limitlessness.
>
> (Chalier, 2002, p. 108)

In his philosophical writings, Levinas addressed this problem by saying that as long as there are only two, the other's need transcends me utterly. My hospitality transforms me into hostage (these two words have the same root in the romance languages). (For some, deeply concerned about the climate crisis but feeling paralyzed, the problem of traumatism addressed in Chapter 1 arises here.) But as soon as there are three or more, the question of justice arises. Then we need laws and contracts and agreements—all those structures that manage limits.[14]

So, can we psychotherapists simply say to the shattered sufferer who arrives that we offer only bread and vegetables? Forty-five minutes, and see you next week? A few dollars to the Sierra Club and now I am an environmentalist? No, of course not. Long ago a patient, brilliant but always hovering on the edges of madness, protested to me that everything about psychotherapy and psychoanalysis was arranged for the protection and convenience of the clinician, and had nothing to do with needs of patients. Only after I invited him to help me design something that might better meet his needs, and to try things out for a while—now I might say I opened at least two sides of my tent—did we settle into fairly conventional treatment for many years. Before then, we walked on the nearby beach, sat in coffee shops—anything to reduce his sense of weirdness.

But because we work with many patients, each with special needs of his or her own, and are limited human beings ourselves, ever more so each month and year, we must, like the rabbi's son, set contracts in advance for time, place, and payment, and work out the rest as best and hospitably as possible in a spirit of welcome, a tent-open spirit. Otherwise they too may notice the closed-off spirit, and turn away in despair once more, just as our southern neighbors have done until recently in the face of northern indifference to the climate problem.

Jacques Derrida raised these complex questions in even sharper form. Derrida, who saw clearly what Levinasian ethics would politically require—open borders, the tent open on all sides—also saw the impossibility. He grew up much exposed to anti-Semitism in Algeria, and thus knew exclusion well. His graveside oration "Adieu to Emmanuel Levinas" is published with a long and longing essay on hospitality, entitled "A Word of Welcome." He explained that welcoming the other with an open door means submitting oneself to the other, making oneself receptive and teachable.

Soon, however, the complications and ambiguities begin to emerge. If only we could simply open our door and heart to all in need as the Abrahamic "law of hospitality" commands. But the conditional "*laws* of hospitality" always conflict with, indeed radically oppose, the unconditional law of hospitality. According to these conditional laws, you may come in only when invited; you must behave well according to local customs when you are inside. You must accept just what is provided, not asking for more. You must already speak, or quickly learn, the local language, and not expect yours to be learned or to be understood by your hosts. You must contribute to the local economy, and keep a low profile, disappearing into the local culture. And so on. Above all, you must not be other, or have needs that might call on the unconditional hospitality. The conditional hospitality is a system that maintains itself in a tenuous balance prior to the arrival of the uninvited foreigner, the Levinasian widow, orphan, and stranger. Emergencies, whether familial or a global migration crisis, facing us with millions whose need is urgent, even desperate but who cannot possibly be expected to meet all these conditions, demand the unconditional hospitality.

Derrida, however, invites us to consider that both types of hospitality may be inextricably linked. In his inimitable style, he begins by drawing our attention to the linguistic ambiguities, beginning with the use, in romance languages, of the same word for guest and host:

> we must be reminded of this implacable law of hospitality: the hôte who receives (the host), the one who welcomes the invited *hôte* (the guest), the welcoming hôte who considers himself the owner of the place, is in truth a *hôte* received in his own home. He receives the hospitality that he offers *in* his own home; he receives it *from* his own home—which, in the end, does not belong to him. The *hôte* as host is a guest. . . . The one who welcomes is first welcomed in his own home. The one who invites is invited by the one whom he invites.
>
> (Derrida, 1999, p. 41)

Let us consider this paradox in our everyday clinical work (easy to extend into cultural pluralism). A suffering person, new or not, arrives to my welcome. Immediately the tables are turned. Nothing happens unless I surrender the leading role, and allow the patient to lead me, to teach me, take me hostage, to inhabit me (as Elizabeth Young-Bruehl reformulates empathy). My welcome creates the possibility that the other may welcome me into her world of loss, confusion, devastation. The welcomer becomes the one who may be welcomed as a lost and wandering stranger. The home I thought I owned was only a way-station, a tent to be opened toward the other who then might in turn share something, some bread of suffering, with me. Any home we seem to possess turns out to be our "common home," the one we have been mindlessly destroying.

So the hospitable one is dispossessed not only of agentic subjectivity—subjectivity becomes subjection and receptivity— but also of possession in the sense that he is king of the castle. Likewise the hospitable clinician, the more "clinical wisdom" she accumulates, and the eco-hospitable human, will live with an ever-diminished sense of control. Like my wise old mother-in-law, who told me she was "learning how to be ninety-eight," not-knowing and not-having will be good enough. It will keep the sides of the tent open for the hungry and strangers.

To keep the tent open today means not only welcoming refu-gees into our countries, and at least temporarily, into our homes, learning their languages, and learning what they need to feel less homeless and bereft. It also means turning a corner on the institu-tional injustices that bring them, that have turned their homes into deserts and war zones. It means reforming our own lives radically, seeing the links between their suffering and our mindless comforts, learning every day. I believe, actually, that only a radical ethics of the fundamental worth of every human life will make the difference we need in the climate crisis. Until we can see, really see, ethically see, that our carbon-hungry "lifestyle" harms, even destroys, the other whose suffering places an infinite responsibility on me, nothing will change, really.

Humanism

We must expect voices to be raised against the perspective I am advocating, serious and thoughtful voices. Above all, many, for example (Smith, 2013), believe that extinction of species consti-tutes an "irredeemable loss, a loss that even eternity cannot rectify"

(p. 21). Like the deep ecologists, Mick Smith believes that prioritizing the suffering of human beings returns us to an irreverent and dominating humanism, including views of human exceptionalism, causing the climate crisis. Smith argues that a post-humanist perspective would dismantle the absolute dividing lines within the natural world. Smith (2013) writes,

> Is a reminder of a multi-species and multi-existent "we" that modern humanism chose to forget, or rather struggled to exempt and/or except the human species from.
>
> (p. 30)

How might a radical ethics respond? Returning to psychoanalysis, to one of its radical and prophetic voices, let us consider Erich Fromm's (Fromm, 1975) definition of humanism, to understand why many environmentalists might think it dangerous, but also to retrieve its value for our moment of crisis:

> Humanism, both in its Christian religious and in its secular, nontheistic manifestations, is characterized by *faith in man, in his possibility to develop to ever higher stages, in the unity of the human race, in tolerance and peace, and in reason and love as the forces which enable man to realize himself, to become what he can be.*
>
> (p. 396, emphasis in original)

Immediately we note the masculinist presumptions, making us suspicious of other smuggled-in forms of hegemony. But Fromm goes on to explain that this tradition, ascendant in the Renaissance, originated in the Jewish tradition in which "if someone destroys an individual, it is as though he destroyed the whole world; and if someone saves an individual, it is as though he saved all of humanity" (p. 397). Solidarity, in Fromm's view, forms the original core of humanism, while reverence for every person's dignity remains indispensable to it. Incompatible with hatred and fanaticism, humanism holds a simple hope in the emergent possibilities of each human and of humankind. It seems to me more than compatible with reverence and care for our shared home. We can be good to each other and to our earth; in fact, the two depend on each other.

And yet, moral conviction, powerful enough to help us now, may require a robust, even a radical, humanism. Human solidarity, as Keith Anderson (Anderson, 2006) notes in comparing Hannah Arendt with Emmanuel Levinas, may be founded on mutual obligation or, alternatively, on radically anarchical (prior to all commitments) responsibility to the widow, orphan, and stranger.[15] This second possibility does not mean a disregard for other species, nor does it disparage contracts and commitments. Instead, without disregarding care for other species, it places a deliberate priority on the needs of the world's poorest humans, as the climate justice theorists we met in Chapter 1, such as Pope Francis and Henry Shue, advocate.

In addition, philosopher J. Aaron Simmons (Simmons, 2012) argues convincingly that we face what he calls a "metaethical emergency" (p. 229), a situation like that facing Britain in 1939 as it considered whether the ordinary laws of war still applied in facing an imminent threat to all civilized life. That we confront, Simmons claims, the looming destruction of a livable world means we do not have the leisure for non-anthropocentric ethics like that favored by the deep ecologists. We must, he believes, immediately prioritize the most vulnerable humans suffering from the effects of climate change if we are to have any chance of motivating the type, extent, and rapidity of change needed. Ordinary ethics, such as the duty and utilitarian theories outlined above, even including deep ecology perhaps, belong to everyday life. "In the context of a metaethical emergency," writes Simmons, "there is no time to advocate theories that do not have a good enough chance of motivating a reasonable public response to the crisis" (p. 232). We have to treat our current situation as an extreme humanitarian emergency, not something to measure against competing ideals and philosophies. Paraphrasing Simmons, emergencies call for a kind of ethical triage that he calls "a hierarchy of ethico-political significance" (p. 230) as he argues for what he further terms "a relational model of anthropocentrism"

(p. 231), essentially the Levinasian response to the face of the suffering other described above. William Edelglass (Edelglass, 2012), in the same vein, writes that "Levinas provides a way of understanding how the singular subject's moral responsibility is the condition for the possibility of collective responsibility" (p. 211). Response to the face of the suffering sister and brother creates political change through prophetic action (Anderson, 2006; Orange, 2016).

But how, privileged as we are, do we come to see and feel ethically, to respond with welcome to the misery of the other, whether we know the stranger or not? Bernasconi (2006) links the visibility of others' enslavement to Levinas's own "memory of servitude." Like all Nazi captives, he had been hungry in a way that no one ever forgets. Do we need to have been that miserable to understand that the condition of humans suffering from persecution and hunger accuses me relentlessly, and places upon me a responsibility without beginning and without end? I hope not, but Judith Butler thinks that, at the very least, exposure to others' suffering helps:

> In the Vietnam war, it was the pictures of children burning and dying from napalm that brought the US public to a sense of shock, outrage, remorse and grief. These were precisely pictures we were not supposed to see, and they disrupted the visual field and the entire sense of public identity that was built upon that field. . . . Despite their graphic effectivity, the images pointed somewhere else, beyond themselves, to a life and to a precariousness that they could not show. It was from that apprehension of the precariousness of those lives we destroyed that many US citizens came to develop an important and vital consensus against the war. *But if we continue to discount the words that deliver the message to us, and if the media will not run those pictures, and if those lives remain unnamable and ungrievable, if they do not appear in their precariousness and their destruction, we will not be moved.* We will not return to a sense of ethical outrage, that is, distinctively, for an Other, in the name of an Other.
>
> (2004, p. 150, emphasis added)

Just as we finally came to see as ethically intolerable the misery we were creating in Vietnam, we must help each other to see the connections, to make the links between our prodigal dumping of carbon into the atmosphere, and the human wretchedness our mindless consumption creates.

We might also note that placing human misery at the center of our climate crisis considerations may not violate the injunctions in Asian religions against harming other creatures. No one can do no harm at all; even vegetarians and vegans eat organic things, doing as little harm as possible. Implicitly we recognize a hierarchy of needs, with creatures claiming our reverence all up and down the line. We humbly acknowledge our impact on all the others, as we take to survive. Nothing and no one is innocent. This attitude radically inverts the compulsive consumption that ignores our effects on the poorest humans, on other species, and on our planetary home.

Simmons's "anthropocentric" position, mine as well, depends on seeing that we truly face an emergency that menaces not only suffering human beings now, but the possibility of livable human life on this planet. The threat of Hitler, more visible as his *Wehrmacht* rolled over one country after another, dominating a continent, felt more real than our imminent tipping points. Journalists, climate scientists, and the media who broadcast their stories, become the true heroes and heroines now, placing their lives and reputations at stake to tell us of ocean destruction, of rising oceans eliminating the homes of island people, of starving and war-ravaged people seeking shelter. They help us to make connections among these phenomena. More journalists die every year helping us to see beyond the confines of our comfort, and to link these others as our kin. Judith Butler has worried that media vacuity hides precarity (Butler, 2004, 2009); I agree heartily, but also note journalism's power to make human vulnerability visible, confronting us with our responsibility, placing us in question. "Nothing is nobler than exposing man's [sic] misery" (Levinas & Robbins, 2001, p. 190).

Simmons believes our current crisis merits extreme response, both theoretically and practically. Though he concerns himself with theoretical grounds for ethical practice, I am reminded of the saying attributed to several thinkers: "there is nothing so practical as a good theory." We need to know *why* we prioritize the relief of human misery, even knowing that other species and natural features matter too. We need to know *why* we save every drop of water: not only because drought is ugly, but because our neighbors have no drinking water. We need to know *why* we object to mountain-top coal mining: not only because it creates an awful landscape, but because it makes our air unbreathable, adds significantly to the global warming threatening us all but most urgently the poorest, and menaces the health of all who work with coal.

An anthropocentric ethic to confront change and address climate justice does not exclude the worries so central to other approaches. Changing our lives to respond to the suffering of others will also mean living simply and reverently in our common home, with what his namesake, St. Francis of Assisi, understood as our brother and sister species. Anthropocentric ethics means no irreverent rejection of creation, mother nature, or however we find ourselves referring to this home. It does mean looking urgently, immediately, for means, all along the spectrum from "natural" to technological, to relieve suffering in renewable ways. Feeding the hungry, perhaps the aging Levinas's central concern, depends on sustainable, earth-friendly agricultures like those developed by Vandana Shiva and Wes Jackson, cited in Chapter 1. In other words, radical ethics, anthropocentric only because it recognizes the extremity of the emergency in which we find ourselves, not mindlessly reactive but mindfully responsive, looks for every creative way to address the vulnerability created by climate change. Then it evaluates solutions according to how they relieve and empower the poorest, and to how quickly they can come online. Radical ethics finds a place for both individual and collective action at every moment. It finds no excuses for the bystander.[16]

Dissenters, good and thoughtful people, will argue that radical Levinasian ethics, too much corrupted by masculinism,[17] cannot serve to ground climate ethics. Roger Gottlieb (R. Gottlieb, 1994;

R. S. Gottlieb, 2014), for example, wonders whether his "whole edifice would come crashing down if he [Levinas] realized that it is possible to see human identity as based in a relation to the other *from the start*" (emphasis Gottlieb's). The rigid masculine perspective, thinks Gottlieb, prevented Levinas from seeing "our sense of belonging to nature as system, as interaction, as interdependence, which can provide the basis for an ethics appropriate to the trauma of ecocide" (2014, p. 40). Thus Levinas, he thinks and I agree, excludes just what Gottlieb understands as "deep ecology." I, contrariwise, hear Levinas as understanding our pre-original relatedness and responsibility for each other in an even more fundamental way: I am my other's keeper. This is the Levinasian (and Dostoevskian) answer to the much misunderstood biblical command to "have dominion over them." I would also note that feminist opinion on Levinas is much divided. In addition, both Merold Westphal (2008) and I regard Levinas as kin to the moral thinking of Carol Gilligan (Gilligan, 1982), teaching us to prioritize an ethic of care over an ethic of abstract distributive justice. Judith Butler, a feminist philosopher of no mean stature, relies heavily on the work of Levinas in her recent work, seems little worried by his putative masculinism, given the attention he drew to the precarious lives who starve from the effects of our affluent living.

To address the crisis we are living, we must come to feel the destitution of homeless, starving, and persecuted others as our own persecution, "the irreparable wounding of the Self in the Me accused by the other to the point of persecution" (Levinas, 1981, p. 15). David Kleinberg-Levin (Kleinberg-Levin, 2005) explains that

> the accusation of persecution which is inscribed prior to consciousness in the depths of the flesh always becomes, *at the level of consciousness*, an inevitable "persecution" of conscience, a burden that forever holds us hostage. We are *persecuted* by the accusation. We are relentlessly pursued by its exigency—by a responsibility and an accusation from which we can never be released.
>
> (pp. 208–209)

After his return from Auschwitz, Primo Levi (1986, 1988) described a kind of shame for others' crimes, a shame he felt and saw in others, that "man, the species man, we in short, are capable of constructing an infinite enormity of pain" (1988, pp. 85–86). The capacity to feel this shame, found more often in the victims than in the perpetrators and bystanders, becomes essential to the solidarity in the persecution Levinas explains. To take on our pre-primordial responsibility for each other, to take on the challenges of climate justice, we must find the kind of shame Levi describes in the face of others' suffering.

We miss this shame in Cain's insolent response: I do not know: am I my brother's keeper? Without mentioning Cain's murderous violence, the question, "Where is Abel your brother?" comes to him as a gracious invitation to repentance and repair. Cain shamelessly refuses its underlying premise of responsibility, and models not only the "we knew nothing of the extermination camps," but also the "send them back where they came from—this is our country." If they aren't smart enough to get rich from oil, fracking, and coal, too bad for them. In the face of such attitudes, rampant in Europe and North America, only a robust solidarity, enacting our answer to Cain, can begin to solve the problems of climate justice. We can make common cause with romantics who love the earth and its many species—I do myself, as a native Oregonian—but fundamentally we must find ourselves as our other's keepers.

James Hatley (2005), meditating on the story of Cain, notes that outrage solves nothing. Instead, writes Levinas, "the word *I* means *here I am [hineni]* answering for everything and for everyone" (Levinas, 1981, p. 114). I become myself, not as an egoistic monist, but through the other. We can remember here also the African ethics of *Ubuntu*, well explained by Archbishop Desmond Tutu:

> A person with Ubuntu is open and available to others, affirming of others, does not feel threatened that others are able and good . . . knowing that he or she belongs in a greater whole and

is diminished when others are humiliated or diminished, when others are tortured or oppressed.

(Tutu, 1999, p. 31)

Ubuntu, both a sense of human solidarity and a fundamental attitude that becomes a virtue, differs from Levinasian substitution, from hyperbolic responsibility, but not by much. Once again we see, as with Asian religions or philosophies, resources to turn us radically away from forgetting the suffering of others.

Conclusions

First, what can we not conclude? Clearly the radical ethics we have been discussing cannot help either psychotherapists or international public policy experts to decide the best road to climate justice: "equal per capita entitlements, rights to subsistence emissions, priority to the least well off, or equalizing marginal costs" (Edelglass, 2012, p. 227; Gardiner, 2011). Nor does it tell us how to move the seemingly unmovable forces of power and money arrayed against climate justice. These same hegemonies prevent us from associating climate change and its effects with social justice. We must look to the wisdom accumulated by those who overturned apartheid, organized the civil rights movement, and finally brought the Vietnam War to a close, as well as to our partners in the indigenous communities so affected by climate devastation, to find our way. Radical ethics does not provide rules, strategies, political philosophy and structures. Instead, it confronts each and all of us with our responsibility, without beginning and without end, inescapable, for our world and for each other.

Radical ethics means that we cannot go on as we did yesterday, self-satisfied that we are doing our best, or shifting our personal responsibility (Edelglass, 2012) onto "the system." The terrified faces of the destitute refugees, of those whose homes are being turned into desert or going beneath the sea, threatened by violence, forbid me to sleep comfortably and command me to respond. Every day I must allow them to persecute me, to pull me out of my comfortable life, to make me non-indifferent. For each of us, response will take its own form, depending on how and where we see the useless suffering and hear the cries, and on what our own health allows. Dale Jamieson, with Henry Shue one of the clearest voices for climate justice, lists seven actions we must take:

- Integrate climate adaptation with development.
- Protect, encourage, and increase terrestrial carbon sinks.
- Encourage full-cost energy accounting.
- Raise the price of GHG emissions to a level that roughly reflects their costs.
- Force technology adaptation and diffusion.
- Substantially increase basic research spending.
- Plan for a new world in which humanity is a dominant force on the fundamental systems that govern life on earth.

(Jamieson, 2014, p. 9)

He further advocates a life of environmental virtues: temperance, humility, mindfulness, and gratitude.

And yet, a radical ethics differs from other similar ethics like that of Jamieson. It never begins and never ends. The face of the suffering other demands response from me before any agreement ever made (yes, I am my other's keeper), and this responsibility continues. "I more than all the others," as both Dostoevsky and Levinas repeatedly wrote. For the extreme situation in which, once again, we find ourselves, perhaps only the ethic of hyperbolic responsibility can shake us out of our complacency. If not to save our own skin, still comfortable enough, am I not my sister's and brother's keeper?

Notes

1. A new collection of essays, *For Our Common Home* (2015), honoring this encyclical, has just appeared.
2. As Theodor Adorno and T. Schröder (2000) warned after World War II: "We may not know what absolute good is or the absolute norm, we may not

even know what man is or the human [*das Menschliche*] or humanity [*die Humanität*]—but what the inhuman [*das Unmenschliche*] is we know very well indeed. I would say that the place of moral philosophy today lies more in the concrete denunciation of the inhuman, than in the vague and abstract attempts to situate man in his existence" (p. 175).

3. Social Darwinists, under the leadership of Herbert Spencer, taught that peoples, groups, and individuals struggle according to the same laws of "survival of the fittest" that apply to plant and animal species. This view has attempted to justify conservative political views and racism. Often thought to have disappeared, social Darwinism lurks beneath laissez-faire economic theories, and many responses to climate change, presuming that those who should survive it will.

4. Like Merleau-Ponty and Wittgenstein, Gadamer wrote one big book, *Truth and Method* (Gadamer, 1989). I will cite it as (TM and page number).

5. See also Adams (2012).

6. Parts of this section are borrowed from Orange (2016) where I have written more about therapeutic hospitality. See also Orange (2011).

7. In a thought-provoking footnote, James Hatley (2005) writes: "The German term, *Verantwortung*, seems preferable here to the English word 'responsibility.' The German word hints at an intensification of response to the point of being utterly taken up in answering what calls one, whereas the English term's etymology suggests that the ability to respond limits the call to respond" (p. 51, n14). "Murder," writes Hatley about Cain in an earlier footnote (pp. 50–51, n11), "is an attempt to escape the address of the other, to render the world as faceless."

8. Granted that Levinas himself failed to speak out against the violence at Sabra and Shatila in 1982, and/or to see his own Eurocentrism and masculinism (Critchley, 2004).

9. We can also understand, as Sylvia Benso (Benso, 2012) writes, why a Levinasian-inflected environmentalism will make little reference to our rootedness in place. She writes: "The theme of the earth is often linked to problematic notions of space, place, land, home, nation, and blood ties. These notions nourish much racist rhetoric in addition to sustaining the I's claims to domination and usurpation of the places of others. . . . For personal, historical, as well as theoretical reasons, Levinas is rightly suspicious of all discourse of a rooting in the earth" (p. 192). Both indigenous peoples and deep ecologists may find this resistance to place talk difficult. Here we need dialogue about different understandings of "our common home."

10. Not all would agree, of course, but I think Levinas means that Judaism, like all the great religions, means to characterize the human condition in general. Here he means that all of us inherit, without our consent, responsibility toward the stranger, near or far.

11. At least, he says, the text does not say "bread of dried vegetables," "like the [bread] we ate during the war" (p. 100)—that is, when he was in captivity.

12. Psychoanalysts sometimes worry about this infinite responsibility under the rubric of moral narcissism, a topic I have addressed at length in Chapter 3 of Orange (2016).

13. Proponents of virtue ethics like Paul Woodruff (2014) would point out, however, that having the right feelings can be a big help, in increasing our ethical capacity and tendency to respond when need faces us.

14. "My responsibility for all can and has to manifest itself also in limiting itself. The ego can, in the name of this unlimited responsibility, be called upon to concern itself also with itself" (Levinas, 1981, p. 128).
15. "The unconditionality of being hostage is not the limit case of solidarity, but the condition for all solidarity" (Levinas, 1981, p. 117).
16. Simmons is careful to note that his anthropocentrism makes no claim to be the best ethical theory, only one that has a chance of inspiring the needed change. He also firmly denies its classification as an instrumentalism, in which everything serves humans. Instead it refocuses our ethical vision on human suffering, as he believes we urgently need to do.
17. Simon Critchley, who first taught me to read Levinas at the New School some 10 years ago and to whom I am endlessly grateful, has just published a new book (Critchley, 2015) continuing the critique he was making then (Critchley, 2004), but now indicting the whole Levinasian project in Irigarian (Irigaray & Whitford, 1991) tones for the gendered (male) character of the ethical subject. I tend to think Levinas developed a maternal subject in his later work (Levinas, 1981), complexifying gender in his ethics. But this is not the place to work this out.

References

Adams, W. H. (2012). *On luxury: A cautionary tale, a short history of the perils of excess from ancient times to the beginning of the modern era* (1st ed.). Washington, DC: Potomac Books.

Adorno, T. W. & Schröder, T. (2000). *Problems of moral philosophy*. Stanford, CA: Stanford University Press.

Anderson, K. (2006). Public Transgressions: Levinas and Arendt. In A. Horowitz & G. Horowitz (Eds.), *Difficult justice: Commentaries on Levinas and politics* (pp. 127–147). Toronto: University of Toronto Press.

Barnhill, D. L., Gottlieb, R. S., & American Academy of Religion. National Meeting (2001). *Deep ecology and world religions: New essays on sacred grounds*. Albany: State University of New York Press.

Benso, S. (2012). Earthly Morality and the Other: From Levinas to Environmental Sustainability. In W. Edelglass, J. Hatley, & C. Diehm (Eds.), *Facing nature: Levinas and environmental thought* (pp. 191–208). Pittsburgh: Duquesne University Press.

Bentham, J. (1876). *An introduction to the principles of morals and legislation*. Oxford: The Clarendon Press.

Bernanos, G., & Morris, P. (1937). *The diary of a country priest*. New York: The Macmillan Company.

Bernasconi, R. (1995). "Only the Persecuted . . .": Language of the Oppressor, Language of the Oppressed. In A. T. Peperzak (Ed.), *Ethics as first philosophy: The significance of Emmanuel Levinas for philosophy, literature and religion* (pp. 77–86). New York; London: Routledge.

Bernasconi, R. (2006). Strangers and Slaves in the Land of Egypt: Levinas and the Politics of Otherness. In A. Horowitz & G. Horowitz (Eds.), *Difficult justice: Commentaries on Levinas and politics* (pp. 246–261). Toronto: University of Toronto Press.

Bernasconi, R. (2010). Globalization and World Hunger: Kant and Levinas. In P. Atterton & M. Calarco (Eds.), *Radicalizing Levinas* (pp. 69–86). Albany: State University of New York Press.

Bookchin, M. (2007). *Social ecology and communalism.* Oakland, CA: AK Press.

Butler, J. (2004). *Precarious life: The powers of mourning and violence.* London; New York: Verso.

Catholic Church Pope (2013– : Francis). (2015). *Encyclical on climate change and inequality: On care for our common home.* Brooklyn, NY: Melville House Publishing.

Chalier, C. (2002). Levinas and the Talmud. In S. Critchley & R. Bernasconi (Eds.), *The Cambridge companion to Levinas* (pp. 100–118). Cambridge, UK: Cambridge University Press.

Critchley, S. (2002). Introduction. In S. Critchley & R. Bernasconi (Eds.), *The Cambridge companion to Levinas* (pp. 1–32). Cambridge, UK: Cambridge University Press.

Critchley, S. (2004). Five Problems in Levinas's View of Politics and the Sketch of a Solution to Them. *Political Theory, 32,* 172–185.

Critchley, S. (2015). *The problem with Levinas* (1st ed.). Oxford, UK: Oxford University Press.

Critchley, S., & Bernasconi, R. (2002). *The Cambridge companion to Levinas.* Cambridge; New York: Cambridge University Press.

Cushman, P. (1996). Disputed Subjects by Jane Flax (New York: Routledge, 1995). *Psychoanalytic Dialogues, 6*(6), 859–874.

Cushman, P. (2005). Between Arrogance and a Dead-End: Psychoanalysis and the Heidegger-Foucault Dilemma. *Contemporary Psychoanalysis, 41,* 399–417.

Cushman, P. (2007). A Burning World, an Absent God: Midrash, Hermeneutics, and Relational Psychoanalysis. *Contemporary Psychoanalysis, 43,* 47–88.

Derrida, J. (1999). *Adieu to Emmanuel Levinas.* Stanford, CA: Stanford University Press.

Devall, B., & Sessions, G. (1985). *Deep ecology.* Salt Lake City, Utah: G.M. Smith.

Edelglass, W. (2012). Rethinking Responsibility in an Age of Anthropogenic Climate Catastrophe. In W. Edelglass, J. Hatley, & C. Diehm (Eds.), *Facing nature: Levinas and environmental thought* (pp. 209–228). Pittsburgh: Duquesne University Press.

Fromm, E. (1975). Humanism and Psychoanalysis. *Contemporary Psychoanalysis, 11,* 396–405.

Gadamer, H.-G. (1982). *Reason in the age of science.* Cambridge, MA: MIT Press.

Gadamer, H.-G. (1989). *Truth and method* (2nd ed.). New York: Crossroad.

Gadamer, H.-G. & Palmer, R. E. (2007). *The Gadamer reader: A bouquet of the later writings.* Evanston, IL: Northwestern University Press.

Gardiner, S. M. (2011). *A perfect moral storm: The ethical tragedy of climate change.* New York: Oxford University Press.

Gilligan, C. (1982). *In a different voice: Psychological theory and women's development.* Cambridge, MA: Harvard University Press.

Gottlieb, R. (1994). Ethics and Trauma: Levinas, Feminism and Deep Ecology. *Cross Currents, 44,* 222–240.

Gottlieb, R. S. (2014). *Political and spiritual: Essays on religion, environment, disability, and justice.* London: Rowman and Littlefield.

Grondin, J. (1994). *Introduction to philosophical hermeneutics.* New Haven, CT: Yale University Press.

Habermas, J. (1984). *The theory of communicative action.* Boston: Beacon Press.

Habermas, J. (1987). *The philosophical discourse of modernity: Twelve lectures.* Cambridge, MA: MIT Press.

Halloy, S., & Lockwood, J. (2007). Ethical Implications of the Laws of Pattern Abundance Distribution. In P. Cilliers (Ed.), *Thinking complexity* (Vol. 1, pp. 99–118). Mansfield, MA: ISCE Publishing.

Hatley, J. (2005). Beyond Outrage: The Delirium or Responsibility in Levinas's Scene of Persecution. In E. Nelson, A. Kapust, & K. Still (Eds.), *Addressing Levinas* (pp. 34–51). Evanston, IL: Northwestern University Press.

Irigaray, L., & Whitford, M. (1991). *The Irigaray reader.* Cambridge, MA: Basil Blackwell.

Jamieson, D. (2014). *Reason in a dark time: Why the struggle against climate change failed—and what it means for our future.* Oxford, UK: Oxford University Press.

Jonas, H. (1984). *The imperative of responsibility: In search of an ethics for the technological age.* Chicago: University of Chicago Press.

Kant, I., Ellington, J. W., & Kant, I. (1983). *Ethical philosophy: The complete texts of grounding for the metaphysics of morals and metaphysical principles of virtue (part II of the metaphysics of morals).* Indianapolis: Hackett Pub. Co.

Kleinberg-Levin, D. M. (2005). Persecution: The Self at the Heart of Metaphysics. In E. Nelson, A. Kapust, & K. Still (Eds.), *Addressing Levinas* (pp. 199–235). Evanston, IL: Northwestern University Press.

Levi, P. (1986). *The reawakening.* New York: MacMillan.

Levi, P. (1988). *The drowned and the saved.* New York: Summit Books.

Levi, P., & Levi, P. (1986). *Survival in Auschwitz; and, The reawakening: two memoirs.* New York, Summit Books.

Levinas, E. (1969). *Totality and infinity: An essay on exteriority.* Pittsburgh: Duquesne University Press.

Levinas, E. (1981). *Otherwise than being: Or, beyond essence.* The Hague; Boston: M. Nijhoff; Distributors for the U.S. and Canada, Kluwer Boston.

Levinas, E. (1987). *Collected philosophical papers.* Dordrecht, The Netherlands; Boston Hingham, MA, USA: Nijhoff; Distributors for the United States and Canada, Kluwer Academic.

Levinas, E. (1988). Useless Suffering. In R. Bernasconi & D. Wood (Eds.), *The provocation of Levinas: Rethinking the other* (pp. xii, 194). London; New York: Routledge.

Levinas, E. (1990). *Nine Talmudic readings.* Bloomington: Indiana University Press.

Levinas, E. (1996). *Proper names.* Stanford, CA: Stanford University Press.

Levinas, E., & Nemo, P. (1985). *Ethics and infinity* (1st ed.). Pittsburgh: Duquesne University Press.

Levinas, E., Peperzak, A. T., Critchley, S., & Bernasconi, R. (1996). *Emmanuel Levinas: Basic philosophical writings.* Bloomington: Indiana University Press.

Levinas, E., & Robbins, J. (2001). *Is it righteous to be? Interviews with Emmanuel Levinas.* Stanford, CA: Stanford University Press.

Macy, J., & Johnstone, C. (2012). *Active hope: How to face the mess we're in without going crazy.* Novato, CA: New World Library.

Mill, J. S. (1970). *The subjection of women.* New York: Source Book Press.

Mill, J. S. (2007). *Utilitarianism.* Mineola, NY: Dover Publications.

Naess, A., Drengson, A. R., & Devall, B. (2008). *Ecology of wisdom: Writings by Arne Naess.* Berkeley: Counterpoint; Distributed by Publishers Group West.

Naess, A., & Sessions, G. (1993). *Clearcut: The tragedy of industrial forestry* (B. Devall Ed.). San Francisco, CA: Sierra Club and Earth Island Press.

Orange, D. (2009). Intersubjective Systems Theory: A Fallibilist's Journey. In N. VanDerHeide & W. Coburn (Eds.), *Self and systems: Explorations in contemporary self psychology* (pp. 237–248). Boston: Blackwell.

Orange, D. (2016). *Nourishing the inner life of clinicians and humanitarians: The ethical turn in psychoanalysis.* London; New York: Routledge.

Orange, D. M. (1995). *Emotional understanding: Studies in psychoanalytic epistemology.* New York: Guilford Press.

Orange, D. M. (2010). *Thinking for clinicians: Philosophical resources for contemporary psychoanalysis and the humanistic psychotherapies.* New York: Routledge.

Orange, D. M. (2011). *The suffering stranger: Hermeneutics for everyday clinical practice.* New York: Routledge, Taylor & Francis Group.

Rawls, J. (1971). *A theory of justice.* Cambridge, MA: Belknap Press of Harvard University Press.

Rawls, J., & Kelly, E. (2001). *Justice as fairness: A restatement.* Cambridge, MA: Harvard University Press.

Ricoeur, P. (1992). *Oneself as another.* Chicago: University of Chicago Press.

Sartre, J.-P. (2001). *Being and nothingness.* New York: Citadel Press.

Scheibler, I. (2000). *Gadamer: Between Heidegger and Habermas.* Lanham, MD: Rowman & Littlefield Publishers.

Schumacher, E. F. (1973). *Small is beautiful: Economics as if people mattered.* New York: Harper & Row.

Simmons, J. (2012). A Relational Model of Anthopocentrism: A Levinasian Approach to the Ethics of Climate Change. In W. Edelglass, J. Hatley, & C. Diehm (Eds.), *Facing nature: Levinas and environmental thought* (pp. 229–252). Pittsburgh: Duquesne University Press.

Singer, P. (1975). *Animal liberation: A new ethics for our treatment of animals.* New York: New York Review; Distributed by Random House.

Singer, P. (2004). *One world: The ethics of globalization* (2nd ed.). New Haven, CT: Yale University Press.

Smith, M. (2011). *Against ecological sovereignty: Ethics, biopolitics, and saving the natural world.* Minneapolis: University of Minnesota Press.

Smith, M. (2013). Ecological Community, the Sense of the World, and Senseless Extinction. *Environmental Humanities, 2,* 21–41.

Stern, D. B. (1990). Courting Surprise—Unbidden Perceptions in Clinical Practice. *Contemporary Psychoanalysis, 26,* 452–478.

Stern, D. B. (1991). A Philosophy for the Embedded Analyst—Gadamer's Hermeneutics and the Social Paradigm of Psychoanalysis. *Contemporary Psychoanalysis,*
27, 51–80.

Stern, D. B. (1997). *Unformulated experience: From dissociation to imagination in psychoanalysis.* Hillsdale, NJ: Analytic Press.

Stern, D. B. (2005). The Man Who Mistook His Impact for a Hat: Reactions to the
Interview of Levenson. *Contemporary Psychoanalysis, 41*, 691–711.

Tutu, D. (1999). *No future without forgiveness* (1st ed.). New York: Doubleday.

Westphal, M. (2008). *Levinas and Kierkegaard in dialogue.* Bloomington: Indiana
University Press.

Woodruff, P. (2014). *Reverence: Renewing a forgotten virtue* (2nd ed.). New York:
Oxford University Press.

Afterword
Thoughts after Paris: climate solidarity

The Paris climate talks, COP21, much anticipated and justly celebrated, occurred just after I sent the main text of this small volume to my publisher. The "Parties" agreed, for the first time, to work toward a 1.5 degree limit on warming of the planet, a better result than most observers expected, and built a framework of targets for decarbonizing, and assisting the adaptation of the poorest to damage already done and coming. They rightly celebrated. But as many have observed, the work remains to be done. No one should think we can now leave this problem to governments and experts, much as we need them. Nothing I can see has changed since the Paris talks, except that climate has disappeared from the front pages of the news. So where does Paris leave us with climate justice, psychoanalysis, and radical ethics?

Questioning borders

Colonialism, the heritage of the United States, Canada, Australia, and several other so-called developed nations, means that we privileged ones live on land stolen from indigenous peoples, few of whom remain to say anything about our crimes, and whose voices we rarely hear. Only recently have some begun to question the celebration of Columbus Day, newly realizing that it memorializes the beginning of a genocide. I live myself in an extraordinary retirement community devoted to peace, justice, and climate care, but we call ourselves Pilgrims, as if innocent of colonial crimes. I live on Mayflower Road! How can we justify keeping refugees, fleeing from chaos our country has engendered in Central America, or from the Middle East, as if we were entitled to possess this land? Returning to radical ethics, the suffering of others "puts in question the world possessed" (Levinas, 1969, p. 173).

Equally unconscious, I did not understand until recently how much the industrial revolution, with its intricate dependence on international trade and growing consumerism in the 18th and 19th century, depended on African slavery. "Needs" developed for coffee, tobacco, indigo, sugar, and cotton. The freedom so prized in our fledgling democracy extended only to the privileged white males. Making this history visible, linking this history to the misery climate injustice wreaks on the darker-skinned poor to this day, could create a shocking gestalt shift in our ethical consciousness.

Undoubtedly, this perspective—seeing carbon-and-methane living of the relatively affluent as racist and as requiring a turn to a radical ethic of responsibility—is only one perspective on the climate emergency most of us keep evading. I offer it as the contribution I am able to make at this moment to a needed conversation, especially hoping my colleagues in philosophy and psychoanalysis will take up the challenge and offer other ways to get us all moving toward a future where we live as brothers and sisters in our common home.

References

Davis, D. B. (2006). *Inhuman bondage: The rise and fall of slavery in the New World*. New York: Oxford University Press.

Levinas, E. (1969). *Totality and infinity: An essay on exteriority*. Pittsburgh: Duquesne University Press.

Appendix I
UN Declaration on Climate Justice

"All human beings are born free and equal in dignity and rights."
(UN Declaration of Human Rights)

Our vision

As a diverse group of concerned world citizens and advocates, we stand in defense of a global climate system that is safe for all of humanity. We demand a world where our children and future generations are assured of fair and just opportunities for social stability, employment, a healthy planet and prosperity.

We are united in the need for an urgent response to the climate crisis—a response informed by the current impacts of climate change and the science that points to the possibility of a global temperature increase of 4°C by the end of this century. The economic and social costs of climate impacts on people, their rights, their homes, their food security and the ecosystems on which they depend cannot be ignored any longer. Nor can we overlook the injustice faced by the poorest and most vulnerable who bear a disproportionate burden from the impacts of climate change.

This reality drives our vision of climate justice. It puts people at the centre and delivers results for the climate, for human rights, and for development. Our vision acknowledges the injustices caused by climate change and the responsibility of those who have caused it. It requires us to build a common future based on justice for those who are most vulnerable to the impacts of climate change and a just transition to a safe and secure society and planet for everyone.

Achieving climate justice

A greater imagination of the possible is vital to achieve a just and sustainable world. The priority pathways to achieve climate justice are:

Giving voice: The world cannot respond adequately to climate change unless people and communities are at the centre of decision-making at all levels—local, national and international. By sharing their knowledge, communities can take the lead in shaping effective solutions. We will only succeed if we give voice to those most affected, listen to their solutions, and empower them to act.

A new way to grow: There is a global limit to the carbon we can emit while maintaining a safe climate and it is essential that equitable ways to limit these emissions are achieved. Transforming our economic system to one based on low-carbon production and consumption can create inclusive sustainable development and reduce inequality. As a global community, we must innovate now to enable us to leave the majority of the remaining fossil fuel reserves in the ground—driving our transition to a climate resilient future. To achieve a just transition, it is crucial that we invest in social protection, enhance worker's skills for redeployment in a low-carbon economy and promote access to sustainable development for all. Access to sustainable energy for the poorest is fundamental to making this transition fair and to achieving the right to development. Climate justice also means free worldwide access to breakthrough technologies for the transition to sustainability, for example, efficient organic solar panels and new chemical energy storage schemes.

Investing in the future: A new investment model is required to deal with the risks posed by climate change—now and in the future, so that intergenerational equity can be achieved. Policy certainty sends signals to invest in the right things. By avoiding investment in high-carbon assets that become obsolete, and prioritizing sustainable alternatives, we create a new investment model that builds capacity and resilience while lowering emissions. Citizens are entitled to have a say in how their savings, such as pensions, are invested to achieve the climate future they want. It is critical that companies fulfil their social compact to invest in ways that benefit communities and the environment. Political leaders have to provide clear signals to business and investors that an equitable low-carbon economic future is the only sustainable option.

Commitment and accountability: Achieving climate justice requires that broader issues of inequality and weak governance are addressed both within countries and at a global level. Accountability is key. It is imperative that Governments commit to bold action informed by science, and deliver on commitments made in the climate change regime to reduce emissions and provide climate finance, in particular for the most vulnerable countries. All countries are part of the solution but developed countries must take the lead, followed by those less developed, but with the capacity to act. Climate justice increases the likelihood of strong commitments being made as all countries need to be treated fairly to play their part in a global deal. For many communities, including indigenous peoples around the world, adaptation to climate change is an urgent priority that has to be addressed much more assertively than before.

Rule of law: Climate change will exacerbate the vulnerability of urban and rural communities already suffering from unequal protection from the law. In the absence of adequate climate action there will be increased litigation by communities, companies, and countries. International and national legal processes and systems will need to evolve and be used more imaginatively to ensure accountability and justice. Strong legal frameworks can provide certainty to ensure transparency, longevity, credibility and effective enforcement of climate and related policies.

Transformative leadership

World leaders have an opportunity and responsibility to demonstrate that they understand the urgency of the problem and the need to find equitable solutions now. At the international level and through the United Nations, it is crucial that leaders focus attention on climate change as an issue of justice, global development and human security. By treating people and countries fairly, climate justice can help to deliver a strong, legally binding climate agreement in 2015. It is the responsibility of leaders to ensure that the post-2015 development agenda and the UNFCCC climate negotiations support each other to deliver a fair and ambitious global framework by the end of 2015. Local and national leaders will implement these policies on the ground, creating an understanding of the shared challenge amongst the citizens of the world and facilitating a transformation to a sustainable global society.

As part of global collective action, greater emphasis should be given to the role of diverse coalitions that are already emerging at the community, local, city, corporate, and country levels and the vital role they play in mobilizing action. These coalitions are already championing the solutions needed to solve the crisis and their effect can be maximized by supporting them to connect and scale up for greater impact.

Climate justice places people at its centre and focuses attention on rights, opportunities and fairness. For the sake of those affected by climate impacts now and in the future, we have no more time to waste. The "fierce urgency of now" compels us to act.

Appendix 2
Online resources

Science

www.ipcc.ch/index.htm
www.iea.org
www.tyndall.ac.uk/
www.noaa.gov/
www3.epa.gov/climatechange/ghgemissions/gases/ch4.html

Ethics and politics

www.ecobuddhism.org/bcp/all_content/buddhist_declaration
www.sierraclub.org/
www.climatepsychologyalliance.org/
www.350.org

Index